G80502643

THE
INDUSTRIAL SOCIETY

Three Essays
on
Ideology and Development

RAYMOND ARON

A Clarion Book

PUBLISHED BY
SIMON AND SCHUSTER

A CLARION BOOK
PUBLISHED BY SIMON AND SCHUSTER
ROCKEFELLER CENTER, 630 FIFTH AVENUE
NEW YORK, NEW YORK 10020
ALL RIGHTS RESERVED
INCLUDING THE RIGHT OF REPRODUCTION
IN WHOLE OR IN PART IN ANY FORM
COPYRIGHT© 1967 BY FREDERICK A. PRAEGER, INC.
SECOND PAPERBACK PRINTING
REPRINTED BY ARRANGEMENT WITH FREDERICK A. PRAEGER, INC.

Published in France in 1966 by Librairie Plon in the collection "Preuves" under the title *Trois essais sur l'âge industriel*.

Chapter I is a revised version of an English translation published by *Encounter* in June 1964 under the title "The Epoch of Universal Technology."

SBN 671-20804-7

MANUFACTURED IN THE UNITED STATES OF AMERICA
PRINTED BY MURRAY PRINTING CO., FORGE VILLAGE, MASS.
BOUND BY ELECTRONIC PERFECT BINDERS, INC., BLOOMFIELD, N.J.

Contents

The Industrial Society

Introduction

The three essays collected in this book deal with the same problems but approach them from different angles. The circumstances of composition explain the approach adopted in each particular case.

The first, "Development Theory and the Ideological Problems of Our Time," was written in 1962, on my return from a visit to Brazil. It is an expanded version of a lecture I delivered there before university audiences, whose reactions were both typical and instructive. Ideas that seemed obvious to me—e.g., the state of high development of some countries is neither a cause nor a condition of the underdevelopment of other countries—were accepted in some places, rejected in others, and everywhere caused surprise. Therefore, this first essay is centered less on development theory in itself than on the link between the various phases of development and a particular way of interpreting our times.

The second, "Development Theory and Evolutionist Philosophy," was written a year earlier, in 1961, for a symposium organized by UNESCO and the École Pratique des Hautes Études. It is in the nature of a reply to a report presented by Professor Morris Ginsberg and based on what is called the evolutionist philosophy of history, according to which the *total* future of mankind is subject to a law of increasing rationality and morality. Consequently, this essay is centered on the distinction between *rationality* (whether scientific, technical, or administrative) and *historical reason.*

The third essay, "The End of Ideology and the Renaissance of Ideas," written in 1964, is meant to counteract certain assumptions connected with industrial society and the end of ideologies. The widespread discussion of these themes has caused certain misunderstandings that I should like to dispel by putting forward my own interpretation. When, some ten years ago, I began a comparative study of the Soviet-type and Western systems in their economic, * social, † and political ‡ aspects, I never imagined that similarities would be taken to signify identity or that, a few years later, there would be a tendency to underestimate the importance of the differences or to suppose the inevitable convergence of hostile systems in an intermediary form dubbed "social democracy."

* *Dix-huit leçons sur la société industrielle* (Paris: Collection Idées, Gallimard, 1963).

† *La Lutte des Classes* (Paris: Collection Idées, Gallimard, 1964).

‡ *Démocratie et totalitarisme,* 1965.

This last essay remains on the level of sociological analysis or ideological criticism, but it expresses a philosophical attitude that continues, apparently, to irritate Marxists, existentialists, and Hegelians alike.

The last representatives of Marxism-Leninism of the Stalinist variety—a dwindling school but one that still has a number of members in France—find it intolerable that one should use a basically Marxist method for the analysis of those societies which call themselves socialist. Yet it is quite in keeping with the teachings of Marx to discuss the relations between the Soviet system and the initial phases of the accumulation of capital. The French existentialists, if only as a consequence of their philosophy of commitment, ought to have admitted that their political preferences originate in a decision more or less justified by circumstances but, in the last resort, of a personal nature. However, in their desire to be allied with the Marxist-Leninists, they have, during the last twenty years, devoted great ingeniousness and much specious reasoning to the hopeless task of achieving a synthesis between a philosophy of arbitrary decisions and a philosophy of the total rationality of history. The party they supported was supposed to be the embodiment of good as opposed to evil, of the future as against the past, and to be the instrument of the sublime achievements of history. As for the Hegelians, from their philosophical heights they look down with indifference and contempt on their contemporaries at a time when "political thought has reached its lowest level." *

Like my previous book, *Essai sur les libertés,* these three essays are written in a style which, according to André Fontaine, "is calculated to exasperate these people who refuse to

---

* Eugene Fleischmann, *La Philosophie politique de Hegel* (Paris: Plon, 1964), Preface, p. 1.

look at reality except through the prism of their ambition or ideologies." And I am afraid that Delcroix may be again tempted to write: "How has Raymond Aron achieved the rather sad serenity of his books, when he is interpreting so dramatic a period? There is a large element of mystery in his intellectual virtuosity and in his analysis, which are devoid of both hope and despair." A writer can never solve his own mystery, especially when confession is repugnant to him and he sees something rather indecent in the persistent contemporary tendency to confuse accounts of private life with political reflection. But what *Le Nouvel Observateur* refers to as "the mysteries of Raymond Aron" only appears mysterious in the provincial atmosphere inhabited by left-wing Parisian intellectuals.

Even supposing I have "achieved serenity," which I doubt, the present dramatic period of history would be a sufficient explanation in itself. I was trained by French professors and steeped in Kantian philosophy with the result that, at the age of twenty, I imagined the world to be very different from what it was or what I discovered it to be in Germany in 1930, when a demagogue of diabolical genius was beginning to lead a highly civilized nation in the direction of political adventurism and barbarism. As a Jew who did not perish in the greatest massacre of the innocents of modern times, how can I forget that millions of human beings were slaughtered according to industrial techniques? How can I forget that noble minds and generous spirits acclaimed "the personality cult" and turned a blind eye on the deportation of the kulaks, the great purge, and the liquidation of the Jewish intelligentsia?

Indeed, what seems to me to be mysterious is the mixing of invective with analysis, the ability to move from commitment to universal history and to make pitiless onslaughts on individuals while at the same time demanding total perfection in the society of the future. In so far as Sartre-like political literature is considered normal, the attempt to think with lucidity and detachment, which has always been the ambition of philosophers, must appear mysterious. When I presented my doctoral thesis, one of the members of the examining committee inquired about the private reasons which might account for what he referred to as my "melancholy approach." Such reasons may well have existed, but my reply to him—this was in 1938—was that imminent catastrophe could not inspire mirth in a student of history. These catastrophes are now behind us, and I am more than ever convinced that, over and above the tragedies of the present, one can have faith in a certain conception of human destiny. This faith is not devoid of hope, but I mistrust those hopes which can give murderers a clear conscience.

I

Development Theory and the Ideological Problems of Our Time

FOR THE FIRST TIME, all men now share the same history. Mankind is united by its very conflicts and problems, as well as by its technological skills. Militarily, and to an even greater extent ideologically, the two great world powers are present in Asia and Latin America, on the 38th Parallel in Korea, and in the Caribbean. Passenger planes and bombers take only a few hours to fly from Moscow to Washington; half an hour is all that a rocket needs to go from its launching pad in Russia or America to its target in the other country. And, as if to symbolize the unity of the human race, the same words—"capitalism," "socialism," and "imperialism"—are current everywhere, albeit with varying and sometimes contradictory meanings.

Among these widely used words, there is perhaps one—"development"—that takes pride of place. I can think of no country in either the Northern or the Southern Hemisphere, in the Old World or the New, where it is not in common and even obsessive use, as if it defined the major ambition of contemporary man and represented the goal that all communities have decided on as their first priority.

Although the word "development" is such a favorite term in German, English, Spanish, and Portuguese—no doubt in other languages too—it is not necessarily understood in the same way, nor does it refer to the same task in the United States and in Brazil, in Guinea and in France. This essay is prompted by the almost inescapable contrast between the widespread popularity of the word "development" and the diverse problems that development raises in different continents and in different countries. The theory of development may help us to define in what sense mankind is unified by technological skills and their concomitant problems and both divided and unified by questions of ideology.

The modern, or to be precise the contemporary, theory of development stems from three sources, each of which suggests a particular interpretation of the word and the phenomenon: the long-term statistical study of economic growth; the contrast between rich and poor countries (or, to use the common terms, advanced and underdeveloped countries, the latter now being said to be "in process of development"); and, thirdly, the comparison between Soviet and Western economic and social organization.

The first source—the statistical study of long-term economic growth—is to be found in a famous book, the first edition of which appeared in 1940, *Conditions of Economic Progress,* by the Australian economist Colin Clark. Since it came out, many other economists, and in particular the Frenchman Jean Fourastié, have arrived independently at similar conclusions and in some cases have corrected Clark's findings.

It had long been known that modern economies were "in process of development" either because of the growing numbers of workers or because of the increase in individual output. The phenomenon had been recorded, sometimes even described and analyzed, by classical economists; but thirty or forty years ago, specialists did not attach any particular importance to it. It is true that the maturity theory implied, at least partially, a theory of long-term development. It supposed a change in the nature of development according to the stage reached, with opportunities for profitable investment becoming rarer with the aging of the economy. But the maturity theory was based on analysis of short-term or medium-term developments. It was the experience of the great depression that prompted numerous economists, including John Maynard Keynes and Alvin Hansen, to speculate about certain aspects of the phenomenon known as maturity. As we should put it today, they raised the question whether, beyond a certain point, development did not tend to be more or less paralyzed within the framework of a private economy (characterized by market mechanisms and individual decisions about investment made by entrepreneurs). Nowadays, long-term considerations are taken into account directly, not as a by-product of the analysis

of crises and of short-term issues; economic change from century to century, over and above short-term or medium-term
fluctuations, has become a subject of study and of theorizing
and, by the same token, a field for action.

The studies of Clark and Fourastié give a quantitative and
unilinear representation of development. If we take the total
national output of the various countries and divide it by the
number of inhabitants or workers, we get, in each case, the
output per inhabitant or per worker; and it is an easy matter to
put the different countries in an ascending scale of prosperity,
ranging from the underdeveloped countries at the bottom,
with a national income of less than $100 per person per year,
to those at the other end in which the corresponding figure is
over $1,500 or as much as $2,000. As the per-capita income
shows a fairly regular increase, the figure for France in 1960
might be the same as the American figure of a few decades
earlier. If economic progress is defined by the per-capita increase in annual income, the same point will be reached by
various countries at different dates.

Studies of this kind inevitably suggest a simple idea of development, equating it with growth and progress. The three
concepts are still not clearly distinguished in economic writing.
I shall apply the term "growth" to the global or per-capita
increase in the material output; "development" to this increase
when it is the result of changes affecting more or less the
whole of the economy, and "progress" to development when it
seems to correspond to the ultimate aims of the economy. If
the three concepts are confused and total output is taken as the
only criterion of development and growth, the result is a single-
strand view of historical change as tending toward one and
only one end. All countries are seen as taking part in the same

race; some were early starters, others late starters; their speed is measured by their rate of growth, and all of them will, eventually, reach the same goal.

The second source of modern development theory suggests a partly different interpretation and corrects the excessive simplicity and the overquantitative nature of the previous interpretation. In economic analyses, the disparity in output per person between Guinea and the United States, or between India or China on the one hand and West Germany or Great Britain on the other, is usually expressed in figures that indicate a total of so many dollars for one country and so many for another. But any observer realizes that these quantitative differences are symptomatic of qualitative differences. The organization of labor and the instruments of production are fundamentally different, and so is the distribution of manpower between various kinds of work: agriculture, industry, and commerce.

It is true that studies of long-term economic growth, such as Clark's or Fourastié's, popularized the idea of the transfer of manpower from the primary to the secondary and tertiary sectors. Quantitative growth depends on the reduction of the primary sector (agriculture, or agriculture and mining) in favor of the secondary (manufacturing industries) and the tertiary (trade, public services, art, leisure pursuits, and education). According to Clark, the inequality in reward from sector to sector explains the transfer of manpower. According to Fourastié, the unevenness in the speed of technical progress, when one sector is compared with another, and the different rates at which the saturation point is reached in satisfying primary and secondary needs, explains the dwindling amount of manpower employed in the primary sector and, at a later stage, in the secondary sector.

But these shifts in manpower and the changing size of each of the three sectors are, nevertheless, quantitative expressions of more profound, and essentially qualitative, phenomena. For there to be movement from a traditional society and an undeveloped economy—China, India, Guinea, Nigeria, northeastern Brazil, or southern Italy—to a modern society and an advanced economy—northern Italy, the state of São Paulo, or the eastern or western seaboards of the United States—there obviously has to be an increase in output per inhabitant and per worker, and in the proportion of labor employed in industry. But the process of industrialization itself would be impossible if there were no expansion in primary and professional education and if the workers were not trained in those rational habits which run counter to immemorial custom and are indispensable for the achievement of a high output.

While the contrast between the underdeveloped and the advanced countries forces us to admit that development signifies not only growth but historical change, movement from one social form to another, a comparison of the Soviet and Western economies leads to the conclusion that many of the phenomena characteristic of development are common to both. The Soviet and American economies, looked at from Asia, are two different versions of the same social form: under the labels of "socialist construction" or "economic development," they both involve industrialization, urbanization, generalized primary education, expansion of secondary and higher education, a trend toward the nuclear as opposed to the extended family, separation between family life and work, between home and place of work, the setting up of large-scale production units, rigorous differentiation of social function, and so on.

I do not wish to pass premature judgment on two questions

which are still being ardently debated: To what extent are the differences arising from the nature of political regimes and ideologies decisive and to what extent of secondary importance? What truth, if any, is there in the belief that the Soviet and Western societies and economies are growing more alike? I merely wish to note that this third source of the modern theory of development suggests, if not a third approach, at least a third starting point or way of posing the problem. In reading Clark and Fourastié, one gets the impression that all societies are traveling the same road toward the same goal. In comparing the underdeveloped with the advanced societies, one is aware of a historical transformation, a human and social revolution, that concerns the whole of mankind and is opening a new chapter in the history of the race. In comparing Soviet society with Western societies, we are led to reflect on the significance of conflicting ideologies and on the similarities that may exist between political systems that sentence each other to death.

It is easy and tempting to look upon development as being merely growth, as an expansion of the *status quo* or as increased output of the same products by the same methods. In actual fact, development consists not only in increasing the quantity of goods but also in producing other products by other means. A modern society is in a state of constant change as well as of constant expansion. Renewal, as well as quantity, is an obsession with it, since the former is inseparable from the latter.

How is one to describe the kind of society to which development leads and which we shall henceforth term modern, industrial, or scientific? Virtually unanimous agreement, it seems to me, has been reached with regard to the social sector in which this change has taken place: I mean the economic sector, and more specifically, in the organization of work. Instead of hand implements, man now has at his disposal more and more complex machines; the amount of energy available per worker makes it possible to increase the worker's output, to revolutionize agriculture and mining so as to satisfy human needs, and to evolve technical devices which solve the age-old problems of housing, clothing, transport, and communication in a variety of ways undreamed of even by utopians. The exploitation of natural resources has to be recognized as a major characteristic of modern society, without precedent at least as regards quantity. At the same time, this technical mastery expresses a new attitude: the will to dominate the natural environment instead of being dominated by it and, in addition, a concern for measurement, rational organization, and forecasting the future.

Measurement—of working hours or output—is basic to that form of procedure which used to be termed capitalist but is now recognized as being characteristic of all modern societies. Measurement leads to the endeavor to produce more in the same time, or to spend less time on producing the same amount, or to produce a more valuable output in less time. But to achieve this ambition quantitatively, it is also necessary to replace the usual methods of work and organization by reflection or calculation, that is, to adopt what Max Weber calls a "rational attitude" or what is also known as rationalization. Quantitative rationalization involves a new approach to the past and the future. The past, as such, is no longer respectable or sacred. The future is no longer looked upon as a repetition of what has gone before or as an inescapable fate. Tradition is no longer enough to ratify authority or institutions. Encouraged by success, men are determined to work out in advance those quantitative factors determining their future, such as the size of a given population, the resources at its disposal, and its living standards. Modern societies are the first ever to justify themselves by their future, the first in which the motto "Man is the future of man" appears not so much blasphemous as banal.

Modern societies are defined first and foremost by their organization of labor; that is, by their relationship to the external world, their use of machinery, the application of scientific methods, and the social and economic consequences of the rationalization of production. It is impossible, in an introductory study, to give a definition of the family, the state, and the nature of culture in modern society (because all three can take various forms). But there is no doubt that they are affected by development and that they show certain similarities in all advanced societies. (For instance, the extended family will tend to become nuclear; the state will operate through a rationally organized and comparatively centralized bureaucracy; culture purveyed to millions through the mass media will gradually drive out local cultures or superimpose itself upon them.)

The developed society thus outlined, spanning various political systems and representing a goal to which all mankind is tending, corresponds in striking fashion to the conception of modern society that Auguste Comte, following Saint-Simon, worked out ten or twenty years before Karl Marx wrote his description of capitalist society. Both of them realized the prodigious increase in the means of production. Both saw the crowding of workers into factories as a symptom of modernity, as an original feature of the social organization that was coming into being. Both believed that the new working methods were at once the cause and the essential characteristic of modern society.

How, then, it may be asked, did positivism and Marxism differ in their interpretation of modern society? The answer, I think, is simple. Comte considered that the conflicts between the owners of the means of production and the workers—that is, between capitalists and proletariat—were no more than the childhood illnesses of industrial society, which would be gradually cured as society progressed. In his view, modern society was industrial because its essential, perhaps even unique, aim was the exploitation of natural resources in order to improve living conditions (this improvement itself being simply a means toward moral progress). To call modern society industrial was not so much to emphasize the transfer of manpower from the primary to the secondary sector, from agriculture to industry, as to stress the industrialization of work in agriculture, as well as in industry proper. Industrialization arises from the application of science and the scientific spirit to the exploitation of natural resources. In this sense, Comte could have called modern society scientific instead of industrial.

According to Marx, on the other hand, the conflict between capitalists and proletariat was the essential phenomenon conditioning the present state of society. So long as this conflict was not radically eliminated through the revolt of the proletariat and the collective ownership of means of production, expansion of the means of production would have the double effect of increasing the poverty of the masses and intensifying the conflicts. The very acuteness of the evil would eventually be a source of good. The class struggle would abolish political systems that prevent the benefits of science being extended to everyone.

The theory of industrial society, as elaborated by Comte, attached little value to differences in political systems because it refused to give importance to the form of ownership. In Comte's opinion, even if the ownership of the means of production remained in private hands, it had nevertheless become a social function. Some individual must be in charge, must administer and control, but henceforth he would carry out these tasks as a delegate or representative of the community. This theory is curiously in keeping with present-day ideas and with the undeniable facts of the present situation, such as the indisputable resemblances between Soviet and Western society, the comparative weakening of the class struggle in the advanced societies (whether of the one type or the other), the change in the significance of, and the part played by, private ownership where it is still in force, and the reinvesting of strong authority in industrial undertakings and in the state in countries where the revolution set out to abolish hierarchical distinctions in function and command.

During the last ten years, the idea of the industrial society has spread over the whole world, although it has not received universal acceptance, since the Russians refuse to believe that East and West have anything in common and consider the two forms of society to be mortal enemies. Although rejected by the Communists, the idea of the industrial society is used by ex-Communists, who see in it a sign of fidelity to Marxism, if not to Stalinism (the resemblance between the means of production in all advanced societies justifies the comparison between societies with different political systems); it is also used in the philosophy of history because, when we put modern society into the general context of historical evolution, it is impossible not to be struck by what is absolutely new in the contemporary situation.

All historical societies consisted of a mass of peasantry with a greater or lesser urban superstructure. (Even the city-states, which might seem at first sight to be urban societies, were no exception.) Modern societies are becoming essentially urban societies with a peasant residue. The United States uses only 7 or 8 per cent of its manpower to feed the whole population, and it does not know what to do with its agricultural surplus. Admittedly, Americans have a very high proportion of ground area per inhabitant. But technical progress in agriculture has been such that the Federal Republic of Germany, with very little space at its disposal (a little over 200,000 square kilometers), provides four-fifths of the food for a population of 55 million people and uses only 10 per cent of its manpower to do so. It is true that half of mankind is still underfed, but this irrefutable fact only goes to prove that industrial society has not completed the advance that Comte had forecast for it a century and a quarter ago. His prophecy was accurate because, although all societies are not yet organized on an industrial basis, all of them aspire to this type of organization. As for those who reject it, consciously or unconsciously they prefer conservatism and death to life and change.

Development theory, as I have just said, is an integral part of scientific doctrines and ideologies in the countries of the Eastern bloc, just as much as in the West. But the evolution of industrial society is interpreted differently, according to whether the theorist bases himself on studies done in the Clark manner or on the controversy about political systems; that is, on whether he considers industrial society as being industrial or capitalist. The fact is that two rival analyses of trends in modern society are now current: the Marxist analysis, which has been more or less brought up to date so as to take into account the events of the twentieth century; and the Clark-Fourastié-Rostow analysis. Rostow's book *The Stages of Economic Growth* brings out the ideological and theoretical implications of the studies devoted to long-term growth of the total national revenue or of the revenue per inhabitant or per worker.

The Marxist analysis presupposes the successive replacement of one regime by another, as explicitly outlined in the *Communist Manifesto* and in the preface to *A Contribution to the Critique of Political Economy*. According to this view, a social and economic system is defined by the ownership of the means of production, insofar as this determines the power relations between the people engaged in work and the exploitation of some by others. The economy of the ancient world is said to have been founded on slavery, that of the Middle Ages on serfdom, and capitalist economy on the wage-earning class. The establishment of socialism would abolish the exploitation of man by man and the appropriation of surplus value by a minority of owners. (Perhaps the Asian mode of production should be considered as well, in which case one would have to take into account the appropriation of surplus value by the civil-servant class or the state bureaucracy, but this addition, although scientifically necessary, is hardly ever mentioned by supporters of the Marxist analysis or, with a few exceptions, by its critics.)

According to this analysis, the function of capitalism is to ensure rapid development of the means of production. ("Accumulate, accumulate, that is the Law and the Prophets.") This development emphasizes the contradictions within the regime and paralyzes it; finally, that regime will be abolished by the revolution of the impoverished masses.

When expressed in these terms, the Marxist analysis obviously does not correspond to the events of the twentieth century. Unless the American system is considered as a socialist one and ownership by big corporations as collectivism (this, after all, might be less contrary to the spirit of Marxism than Stalinism was), it is patent that, so far, no revolution of the Marxist type has followed the expansion of capitalism or the achievement of mature development. The Russian Revolution of 1917 took place in a country where industrial development had been in progress for only thirty years; three years of war led to conditions in which Czarism collapsed and the Bolsheviks were able to come to power. The Chinese Communist Party emerged victorious from a civil war that had begun during the country's first phases of modernization, and Mao Tsetung's troops were recruited more from the peasantry than from the urban proletariat. The countries of Eastern Europe were "converted" to Sovietization through the presence of the Red Army at the end of World War II. And no one would seriously maintain that socialism in Guinea or Cuba is an example of historical movement from capitalism to socialism inevitably brought about by the contradiction between forces and relations of production.

Similarly, without denying the facts, it is difficult to maintain that capitalism has led to increased poverty and to the sharpening of internal contradictions. Since 1945, the growth of Western economies has been more rapid and more regular than it was between the two wars, and it has not been interrupted by the same severe recessions. It is evident that increased production benefits all classes (although in unequal proportions), and the undeniable phenomenon of mass consumption is the simplest and most obvious answer to those dogmatists who believe in the pauperization of the proletariat.*

Not only is the classical Marxist analysis irreconcilable with the historical evidence; it also contains intrinsic weaknesses. An analysis that presents history as a succession of systems implies the primary importance of the infrastructure, which is itself determined by the ownership of the means of production and the social relations resulting therefrom. Now it is clearly untrue that an economy can be adequately defined merely by noting that the means of production are privately owned, if the expression "private ownership" covers small shopkeepers, big industrial combines, and great landowners like those of Spain or Brazil. To say that the economies of the United States, Spain, Iran, and Argentina are all capitalist is not a very instructive statement, because it conceals substantial, perhaps decisive, differences between economies whose only common feature is that they are not governed by Communist parties and tolerate private ownership of the means of production. Within the framework of the private ownership of the instruments of production, and in the absence of total planning, there is room for many variations in forms of production, productivity, private life, and government, so that the application of the concept of capitalism to all non-Soviet societies is devoid of scientific value. The gulf between the capitalism of the captains of industry of the 1880's and the capitalism of the 1960's appears negligible only to the doctrinaires who, on principle, deny the possibility of reforms without revolution.

Similarly, and even more definitely, it is ludicrous to con-

---

* That is, complete pauperization. It has not been demonstrated that Marx believed in complete pauperization. The question of comparative inequalities is too complex to be discussed here.

sider as being socialist in the full sense any society where the means of production are collectively owned, a Communist Party is in power, and a five-year plan is thought indispensable. We know that such a regime may be disgraced by a personality cult or by the violation of socialist legality. We cannot but note that, in all countries which proclaim their Marxist-Leninist faith, representative institutions have ceased to exist and intellectuals have lost their personal liberty. Are we to conclude that authoritarianism or even totalitarianism are necessary concomitants of planning, collective ownership, and the power of the Communist Party? Let us say rather, with scientific caution and so as not to commit ourselves about the future, that collective ownership of the instruments of production is no more adequate as a definition of an economic, and *a fortiori* of a political, system than the application of the term "capitalist" to Western societies.

These remarks seem to me so self-evident, indeed so banal, that I think the real question lies elsewhere. Why has the Marxist analysis retained its popularity throughout the world? Why is it discussed as if it were still valid? I see three possible answers.

In the first place, Marxism, or at least a certain brand of Marxism, has been raised to the dignity of a state philosophy in the Soviet Union. Russia is now one of the two greatest powers in the world; it is a center of attraction, it arouses feelings of sympathy and stirs the hopes of millions belonging to less favored classes in all countries. Ordinary mortals, and even highly cultured men, do not react to a state philosophy as they do to a scientific hypothesis.

At the same time, with the help of a few additional ideas, it is not impossible to bring the analysis and the facts into line, at least superficially. If we agree to give the name "capitalist" to all societies without collective ownership in which the Communist Party does not hold power; if we state as a principle that the anticapitalist revolution will occur at the weakest link in the chain (Trotsky's metaphor), and if we add that the weakest link is to be found in the nascent capitalism of a predominantly quasi-feudal society; if we suppose that colonial or semicolonial imperialism is an inevitable result of capitalist contradictions and that the anti-imperialist revolt is also a necessary result of the exploitation that victimized the underdeveloped countries, then the outstanding facts of our time—the Russian Revolution of 1917, decolonization, and the anticapitalism of the underdeveloped countries—are transposable into Marxist phraseology and seem to confirm its accuracy.

Thirdly—and this is the essential point—while the contradictions of capitalism, pauperization, and increased exploitation of the masses are not to be seen within any given nation, they seem to have been transferred to the international scene in the form of the greater disparity between the rich nations and the poor ones. The latter tend to conclude that Marx was right and that the development of the one kind of country involves, and indeed is paid for, by the underdevelopment of the other.

This optical illusion, which is all the more acceptable to those who suffer from it in that it throws responsibility for their misfortunes on to others, seems to me to be the basic reason for the present popularity of the Marxist analysis. It is not easy to dispel this illusion, for it has roots in the experience of centuries. As long as economies were more or less stationary, as long as wealth was a more or less constant quantity and chiefly constituted or derived from land, precious metals, and commercial profits, the possession of riches by one part of the population meant that another part had to be poor. This is no longer the case when the economy is essentially progressive, the source of wealth is work, and the amount of wealth at the disposal of the community depends on the quality and efficiency of the work done. From year to year, a given community now produces a greater quantity of goods, not at the expense of others but because its manpower is capable of increased output. It may be that the community buys more raw materials from abroad, but it pays for them, and the producer-countries (setting aside for the moment the question of prices) have a better chance of growing wealthy in their turn because of, and not in spite of, the development of others.

It is therefore essential to insist from the start on this obvious yet largely unrecognized point: In the age of industrial society, there is no contradiction between the interests of underdeveloped countries and those of advanced countries. The former can make progress without the latter losing ground. What is more, progress in one quarter helps progress in the others (at any rate, as long as raw materials are abundant and the area available is capable of accommodating and feeding the population). And if these statements seem surprising to Brazilians, say, let them think a moment about the contrasts between the different regions of Brazil. Can it be said that the poverty of the barren Northeast is attributable to the development and comparative wealth of São Paulo? Can it be said that the development of the Northeast would be impossible but for the corresponding impoverishment of São Paulo? The answer is obviously no. The Brazilians of the Northeast may think that São Paulo does not make a large enough contribution to the improvement of the poor states of the Federation; the taxpayers of São Paulo, on the other hand, may be of the opinion that too great a proportion of their taxes is spent on Brasilia and Recife. But no Brazilian, I think, would conclude that the development of the Northeast involves the impoverishment of São Paulo. And indeed, since true wealth depends on efficiency, why should mankind imagine itself to be involved in a struggle to the death when there is no lack of natural resources and all men can be taught to take advantage of them, even if some do not yet know how to do so?

But, it will be said, this abstract and theoretical balance between the development of the less favored countries and the progress of the fortunate ones is not so important as the facts themselves; are the former imperial powers not responsible for the underdevelopment of the ex-colonies? And do the policies of the wealthy countries encourage or hinder the development of the poor countries? Long and detailed studies would be necessary to give an adequate answer to these two questions. I shall merely indicate the direction in which the answers probably lie.

There is a sense in which the responsibility of the colonial powers is undeniable. Since they enjoyed sovereignty and were responsible for governing, they are guilty insofar as they did or did not do certain things. But this truth should not blind us to the differences between the temper of one age and that of another and to changes in ideas and moral values. The belief that the conqueror is responsible for the prosperity of the vanquished is quite a novel one. A century ago, the English ruling class did not feel any such obligation toward its subject peoples. Moreover, even Europeans themselves did not practice a policy of growth consciously and for their own benefit. In the overseas territories, they thought they had done their duty when they had set up an efficient administration, established order, and introduced a small minority of the "natives" to Western science and culture. It cannot be denied that, by so doing, they often brought about a discrepancy between the increase in population and economic growth. But would the situation have been different if the countries reduced to colonial status had retained their independence?

It is very natural that former colonies should be convinced that they would have done better had they always been their own masters; I shall not try to argue that this may not have been so, because the case cannot be proved. Proof would entail a comparison between two strictly similar experiences that differ only in that in one instance independence had been maintained, while in the other it had not. But in all cases where such a comparison might be possible, there are too many variables for any simple, definite conclusion to be drawn. Development has been no better in Thailand (which was never colonized) than in Vietnam or Burma, no better in Liberia than on the Gold Coast or Nigeria. Japan has undergone startling development; China is still backward. (Japan escaped being a field for European ambitions precisely because its ruling class was intelligent and courageous enough to organize its own Westernization, whereas China lived through almost a century of internal troubles and civil wars before the Communist Party subjected it to absolute rule and pitiless discipline.) It is difficult enough to define the difference between what might have been and what actually happened in countries that were subjected to colonial rule in the strict sense of the term; it is still more difficult in the case of those countries that retained their sovereignty according to the legal definition of the term but were dominated by other powers, perhaps even exploited by them. Is North America to blame for the fact that Latin America has lagged behind in the nineteenth and twentieth centuries? Can it be said that American corporations prevented industrialization in areas where they were established? As may readily be imagined, in cases such as these, there is a strong temptation for each party to blame the other. It may be said that the Latin American countries themselves, had they so wished, could have created the industries that they allowed to spring up with the help of American capital. On the other hand, it may be claimed that American capitalists have made excessive profits and in certain instances shipped their gains back home, browbeaten weak governments, and thus contributed to the slowing down of development. The two points of view are not mutually exclusive, and it is only human to prefer one or the other.

Nowadays, the advanced countries vie with each other in proclaiming their intention to come to the aid of the less favored countries—to which the representatives of the latter reply, sometimes with justification, that deeds do not always accord with words and that the terms of trade often result in the exploitation of the producers of raw materials to the advantage of the industrialized economies; that is, in the last resort, exploitation of the underdeveloped by the advanced. I do not underestimate the importance of the phenomenon, but it is a mistake, I think, to believe it to be a deliberate policy on the parts of governments or corporations.

Any country that depends for 50 or 60 per cent of its supply of foreign currency on the sale of a single product, such as coffee, tin, or lead, is certainly in an unenviable position. In the case of agricultural or raw materials, the risk of a glut on the market is always considerable and, since the elasticity of demand is not very great, a comparatively small surplus is enough to cause a serious drop in prices. But it is not easy for governments and corporations, even if we suppose them to be acting with the best will in the world, to control fluctuations in prices and ensure a stable profit.

Two points are basic in this connection. In the first place, no matter what efforts are made to organize world markets in raw materials, countries in process of development should not be dependent on a single product: variety of crops as well as industrialization are indispensable for the prosperity, economic balance, and independence of all countries, and they can only become more so in the future.

The second point, which will not be so readily acceptable, is that highly industrialized countries do not owe their wealth to the low cost of raw materials any more than they owe it to the enslavement or exploitation of colonies. This is not to say that the colonial powers did not draw substantial advantages from their possessions or that favorable rates of exchange are not welcomed by highly industrialized countries. The fact is, however, that they do not depend on these, for they are marginal factors.

The example of the European countries provides eloquent proof of this. Holland, before the war, drew 17 per cent of her national income from Indonesia. She has now lost her empire, and yet she has never been so prosperous or had such a high rate of growth (about 4 per cent per active member of the community between 1950 and 1960). The same is true of France and Great Britain (in spite of the fact that the latter's growth rate during the last ten years has been lower than that of other European countries). Indeed, this stands to reason. For advanced countries, the cost of raw material represents less than 15 per cent of the gross national product. Even violent fluctuations in the prices of raw materials have only a limited effect on the GNP of industrialized countries, which would still remain wealthy even if they had to pay 50 per cent more for certain basic products. At most, a few countries—in particular Great Britain—would have greater difficulty in maintaining their balance of payments. Even then, they could sell more to the producers of primary goods if the prices of those goods were higher.

It follows that the Marxist analysis of economic evolution is no truer as an interpretation of the relationship among nations than it is as an interpretation of relationships between classes. The Western countries are not condemned to extinction through the loss of their empires and the revolt of the under-developed countries. The latter, to ensure their own progress, do not need to declare war on the West, and it is not in their interests to do so. Economic and psychological tensions and conflicts are many and varied, both within nations and between one nation and another, whether the matter at issue is the price of goods and services or the distribution of wealth. But the volume of wealth is no longer a fixed quantity; it expands with the increase in that fraction of mankind capable of applying science to industry. With or without industrialization, there will always be quarrels, but, if reason is allowed to prevail, there will be no death struggle.

W. W. Rostow's analysis of economic evolution is founded, as I have said, not on the nature of the particular system, but on phases of growth. He distinguishes five stages: *the traditional society, the preconditions of take-off, the take-off, the drive to maturity,* and *the age of high mass consumption.*

Rostow's theory has several features to commend it. It replaces the obsession with stages determined by the nature of the socio-economic system (i.e., feudalism, capitalism, socialism) with a conception of stages determined by the level of national income and of industrialization. Combining the results of Clark's studies with suggestions arising from a comparison of the Soviet economy with Western economies, Rostow tries to discover the pattern of development followed by *all* economies in the process of modernization. At the same time, his theory avoids the drawbacks of rigid determinism; it recognizes the variety of policies of expansion in each phase, as well as the many possible choices that present themselves when maturity is reached and then in the period of mass consumption. Nevertheless, I find his theory at once too confining and too vague.

Rostow's concept of the traditional society strikes me as being of little use because it is supposed to be applicable to all underdeveloped communities. All past societies are put into this single category, whether they be the archaic communities of New Guinea, the Negro tribes of Africa, or the old civilizations of China or India. But the only feature these have in common is that they are neither modern nor industrialized. Such a broad concept is not really very useful, and the task of modernization can hardly be said to present the same problems in such different contexts.

As for the second stage—the preconditions for take-off—we may ask whether it really amounts to a separate phase. It is true that the take-off presupposes profound social, psychological, political, and economic changes. But either this second phase is determined by quantitative and economic characteristics (such as the creation of the infrastructure, a rise in agricultural production, and the building of the first factories), in which case the question arises whether it is really different from the third, the take-off proper; or, alternatively, it is a function of political and psychological modernization, i.e., of a new attitude toward work on the part of workers and governments, in which case it is not so much a clearly defined stage in itself as a continuous process that accompanies all phases of growth. (The French governments of the 1930's were still preaching the doctrine of the balance of agriculture and industry and thus betraying their surprising unawareness of the fundamental nature of modernism.) But whichever qualitative and quantitative definition is preferred, this stage must remain hazy in outline because the beginnings of modernization are profoundly different according to whether the advent of industrial society is a spontaneous internal development or a result of contact with the West.

The third stage, the take-off, is said to be a transitional period leading to sustained and cumulative growth; it is supposed to involve the raising of the proportion of the national income devoted to investments to at least 10 per cent of the whole and, in every instance, to be brought about by the rapid growth of certain sectors of industry, e.g., textiles or railways. The problem is to decide whether the take-off, with its three major characteristics—the investing of 10 per cent of the national income, an industrial sector with a rapid rate of growth, and the setting up of an institutional framework adapted to the needs of modernization—can be discerned in the economic history of presently advanced societies. It must be admitted that specialists in French economic history have found nothing to distinguish the years 1830-60 from those before or after. In the case of Great Britain, the take-off is supposed to have begun between 1780 and 1800, maturity to have been reached in 1859, and mass consumption to have begun in 1940. The time lag between maturity and mass consumption is said not to occur in more recent cases, and it is explained by the social and economic conditions of nineteenth-century England, such as the inequality of incomes and the absence of durable consumer goods.

But one may well wonder if the concept of the take-off, which is so difficult to apply to the history of advanced countries, is really appropriate at the present time. Is it true that when investment exceeds a certain proportion of national income, continuous growth is guaranteed? Is there a point beyond which an economy sustains itself in a state of growth as an airplane remains airborne? The experience of the interwar years should not be forgotten, and it should be remembered that the French economy declined in the 1930's, although it had reached maturity in 1910. Too high or too low a birth rate can drag down an economy that was about to soar.

In any case, one may ask to what extent problems and stages are the same in countries which created industrialized society and in those which imported industrialization or imitated it. How far, for instance, can the 1960 take-off of Brazil, carried out with the help of modern techniques and by a population that is increasing at the rate of more than 3 per cent per annum, be compared to the take-off of France in 1830, when antibiotics, refrigerators, and motorcars were unknown. Advances in hygiene increase population pressures, and mass production of consumer goods encourages consumption. The problems may have some points in common, but at the same time they are remarkably unalike.

None of these considerations, with which Rostow would in any case probably agree, refutes his theory. But taken together, they lead to the following methodological conclusions. It would have been preferable to begin by deciding on the nature of the industrial society to which the stages of growth are leading, rather than taking the latter as identical phases of a process of evolution whose trend remains uncertain. A distinction should have been made between spontaneous growth and indirect growth, between the creation and the imitation of industrial society. It would also have been helpful to determine the features common to all societies in process of modernization as well as the different patterns of growth. Lastly, it would have been wise to raise directly the question of the various possible kinds of industrial society.

It is true that Rostow is careful not to claim either that the Soviet Union will become more democratic as it moves into the stage of mass consumption or, on the other hand, that the United States will become more socialist as American capitalism achieves greater maturity. On the contrary, he points out that several possibilities are open to countries which have arrived at a certain stage of development. Once maturity has been reached, a country can choose between an ambitious foreign policy, a welfare state characterized by social regulations, or an improvement in the standard of living. In the stage of mass consumption, its resources are still greater and therefore the margin of choice is broader still. For instance, it can be said that the American nation or, better still, American families have decided to have more children; the resulting "baby boom" has given a new fillip to consumption.

But I think Rostow has not gone far enough in his analysis of different historical alternatives. The Marxists have claimed erroneously that imperialism was a consequence of the contradictions of capitalism and the European wars a consequence of

imperialist rivalries. Rostow is unwilling to see any strict de-
terministic link between the European wars and a particular
phase of growth, but he presents imperialism as one of the
temptations of economic maturity and the raising of the standard of living as a substitute for external ambitions. I think war
and imperialism are permanent dangers, inseparable from an
international system resting upon rival military sovereignties.
It is difficult to decide whether the increased resources, which
are the result of growth, encourage nations in the direction of
pacifism, by providing them with the instruments of prosperity,
or incite them to adopt an aggressive policy by allowing them
to accumulate the means of destruction.

Similarly, Rostow writes: "Communism takes its place . . .
as one peculiarly inhumane form of political organization capable of launching and sustaining the growth process in societies where the preconditions period did not yield a substantial
and enterprising commercial middle class and an adequate political consensus among the leaders of the society. It is a kind of
disease which can befall a transitional society if it fails to organize effectively those elements within it which are prepared
to get on with the job of modernization." Nothing is more
certain than that the Russian Revolution of 1917 occurred
during a period of confusion created by the beginning of modernization. But this is not conclusive proof that a single-party
system is inappropriate to an advanced technological society.
Nor does it alter the fact that once one of the great powers has
been converted to the Communist system and ideology, others
will be carried along the same road, not because of internal
circumstances but because of the influence that a dominant
power can exert.

The growth of each nation has its own history. *A fortiori,* the modernization of human society considered as a unity also has its history which is both unique (*einmalig*) and peculiar (*einzigartig*). The backward nations do not repeat the experiences of the advance guard but are subject to material and moral pressures exerted by highly developed nations. When France was about to "take off," she did not have to consider the respective merits of the Western (European or American), Soviet, Chinese, and Japanese patterns of growth.

In my view, Rostow's attempt to define the "stages of growth," as if every country must go through the same phases and follow the same road, is both premature and methodologically unsound. I should prefer to start from the concept of the industrial society and, after making a rough distinction between an initial stage and a stage of maturity, try to work out the various kinds of premodern situations, as well as the various kinds of patterns and policies of growth.

This analytical and critical use of the theory of development could best throw light on three problems: Which economic or political system best corresponds to the demands of a particular stage? Which type of system is most likely to occur during a particular stage? And thirdly, if it is the case that different countries follow different paths of development, do they tend to resemble each other when the goal has been reached?

The first two questions are quite distinct from each other; except to optimists who invariably suppose, being confident in the rationality of history, that what is most desirable is most likely to happen.

An often expressed opinion is that the Soviet type of political and economic system is the most efficient during the initial stage of development. This opinion, widespread though it is, is nonetheless surprising; or rather, it seems justifiable only if accompanied by a number of reservations. Economically, a system of the Soviet type undeniably has one major advantage and one major defect. We know from experience that it can build factories and transfer surplus agricultural labor to the towns and to industry. But it has nowhere succeeded in reconciling the peasants to collectivization or in curing the comparative shortage of foodstuffs. At the present time, the Chinese population is suffering from general undernourishment, and since 1960 the country has been buying, annually, several hundred million dollars' worth of food, especially cereals, from abroad. The crisis is not so serious in the European Sovietized states, but it exists, as was borne out in Khrushchev's speeches and the 1962 rise in the prices of basic commodities. When the first five-year plan was introduced, the Soviet Government decided on the collectivization of agriculture, perhaps not so much out of doctrinal convictions as out of a desire to increase the proportion of the harvest diverted from the peasantry in order to feed the urban population, which had swollen through the influx of workers to industry. The proportion was, in fact, raised from 15 to about 34 per cent. But, even if we disregard the fact that the declaration of open war on the peasantry caused the destruction of livestock and widespread famine, it is still true today that the collectivist method is inefficient. The amount of produce obtained from the land has increased only slightly, and the peasant small holdings, which represent an absurdly tiny proportion (a few per cent) of the total agricultural area, continue to produce about half the total quantity of meat and dairy products. Russia, which from the outset had a broader agricultural basis than China, has emerged from the collectivization crises and achieved at least a minimum objective. In China, where the initial conditions were much less favorable (a high rate of demographic growth, a less favorable balance between the area under cultivation and the volume of the population, and a tradition of intensive agriculture), there is a threat of shortages, so much so, indeed, that industrial output is no longer advancing but has declined in the last few years.

The advantage of the Soviet system, if growth is considered not as a priority but as an absolute, is on the political level: in the organization of mass education; in the creation of a centralized bureaucracy working on rational principles together with a powerful state authority based on a single party; and in the simultaneous use of compulsion and organized enthusiasm to create and sustain the collective will to develop and to ensure the acceptance of the hardships involved in the building up of a socialist state. I do not underestimate the monuments of steel and concrete which the Soviet planners have finally managed to erect, but the cost has been considerable, so that anyone who remains faithful to the humanist and liberal inheritance of the West may legitimately hope—not only in his own interest but also for the sake of the people directly concerned —that the underdeveloped countries will ensure their economic take-off without modeling themselves on the behavior of Stalin.

Moreover, there is no general reason why the developing countries should be condemned to go through a Soviet phase. Among the preferable alternatives, the most striking example of success is provided by Japan, not merely contemporary Japan—where the annual growth rate of the net national output is higher than 10 per cent (for a number of years it was more than 14 per cent)—but also the Japan of the Meiji Restoration. During that period, under the influence of an enlightened section of the traditional ruling class, Japan modernized its institutions of government, civil service, legal system, schools, and universities. Politically, the regime was authoritarian, but with representative institutions and a gradual broadening of individual and intellectual freedom. Economically, agricultural reform revolutionized the situation of the peasantry, and the capital necessary for industrialization was taken partly from the old landowners and partly from the savings accumulated by all classes. The essential point was the wholesale nature of the change; reforms, such as universal compulsory education and the rationalization of the legal system and civil service, were imposed from above; thanks to the solidarity among the great families involved in business and affairs of state, a class of semipublic, semiprivate entrepreneurs was created. Old attitudes were at once maintained and renewed through a synthesis of traditionalism and Westernization.

In the light of this experience, it should be possible to list the conditions which are necessary everywhere for the take-off to occur. These are: the setting up of a modern state, that is, one in which the civil service and the legislature have been rationalized, where education in the Western style has become widespread, where a class of entrepreneurs has come into being, and where the necessary capital has been accumulated for investment. It is not often that a ruling class surviving from the premodern period shows itself to be capable of such revolutionary dynamism. But it is also clear that various systems—not merely the Communist one—can provide this pattern of conditions.

What is the most likely system? I do not think there is any definite answer to this question. In the nineteenth century, the countries about to "take off" did not show any need for a specifically Soviet technique. Even Czarist Russia had successfully begun to industrialize without resorting to the extreme measures that later characterized the Stalin era. I would not go so far as to maintain, as Rostow does, that Czarist Russia would have successfully resisted the Bolshevik Revolution had the 1914 war not taken place or had it occurred ten years later. But it is not unreasonable to say that ten years later, thanks to the economic progress that was already under way, the Czarist regime would have been very different and less in danger of the kind of collapse, after three years of war, which gave Lenin and his comrades their opportunity.

The probability of a system of the Communist type coming into being no longer depends entirely on internal conditions in the country concerned but also on the world situation. At the beginning of this century, modernism meant political freedom and the existence of a parliament; now it means industrialization and planning. The geographical position of a country and the ideological conditioning of its revolutionaries now determine, and will continue to determine, the system adopted by it, just as much as its basic demographic or economic facts or the needs of development.

Paradoxically enough, confirmation of this argument is supplied by Cuba. Of all Latin American countries, Cuba was one of those that had least need of a revolution on the Soviet model. The island was not overcrowded; in respect of income per inhabitant, it was third in rank among the Latin American countries; it earned some $600 million per year through the export of sugar, and a middle class was springing up in the towns. Illiteracy was still common in the country districts (more than 40 per cent of the population could neither read nor write). It was important that the economy should not depend on a single crop, and it was desirable that industrialization should be carried out through the agency of Cuban capital and entrepreneurs so as to reduce dependence on the United States. But there was no need of any upheaval to ensure the take-off. Even the nationalization of American corporations did not make the break with the United States inevitable.

It was not economic necessity but the dialectics of misunderstanding and hostility and the dynamic force of ideas and personalities, symbolized and expressed by Fidel Castro, that caused the revolution to end in Sovietization, after being actively promoted by the urban middle classes. Observers differ about the degree of blame to be attached to the clumsiness of American policy and to partisan feeling on the part of Castro himself (or Raul Castro and Che Guevara) in the chain of events between 1959 and 1961. Even if one is inclined to think, as I am, that a more understanding policy on the part of the United States would not have altered the outcome, doubt persists and will continue to do so. But whatever interpretation is finally decided upon, it is impossible to disregard the part played by one or more individuals. Fidel Castro, for instance, after he came to power, dissolved all the parties except the Communist Party and refused to provide an organization for his 26th of July Movement. It was he, in the last resort, who decided that he would rather be the first leader of a Soviet Republic in the Western Hemisphere than the founder of a prosperous, liberal, middle-class republic. Megalomania, anti-Americanism, the political "progressiveness" typical of Latin intellectuals whether they are on the banks of the Seine, in Havana, or in Rio de Janeiro—these various tendencies and motives no doubt account for the words and deeds of a man who, whatever the future may hold in store, is responsible for an event which will count in world history.

It may be asked if the present regime corresponds to Cuba's needs as far as modernization is concerned. Only experience will show. For the time being, the regime is faced with considerable difficulties, but they prove little either way as far as technology is concerned. It is self-evident that by substituting dependence on the Soviet bloc for dependence on America, by obtaining all imports from distant countries and bartering the major part of the sugar harvest instead of selling it for dollars, the Castro regime is setting itself a task that is, to say the least, difficult. It is not the technique of modernization which is in question, but a diplomatic policy entailing a break with the Western Hemisphere and integration into the Russian or Chinese bloc.

This brings us to our second question: Which is the most likely system in the initial phase of industrialization? Here again, it is impossible to give a general and definite answer. It can be taken for granted that, in the modern world at least, the first stages of modernization involve a greater degree of state intervention and the playing of a more important part by civil servants and public investment when entrepreneurs and private capital are lacking. It is also unlikely that countries in process of development will manage to combine representative institutions, universal suffrage, and active participation in government on the part of the masses. Where the masses are already active, one or other of the many forms of authoritarian, single-party systems is at least probable. But the unavoidable political and economic features of such a system by no means amount to Sovietization. The chances or the dangers of a revolution of the Soviet type in a country in process of development increase or diminish according to various factors: the international context, the behavior of the ruling class, the composition of the Communist Party, and the part played by individuals and by accidents.

In some areas, anti-Americanism favors the parties that claim to follow the Soviet pattern, since people are misled into thinking that there is some absolute difference between America and Russia and so reject the possibility of intermediary solutions; they translate their dislike of America into sympathy for the Soviet Union. Moreover, present-day intellectual fashions favor planning rather than the free market, industry more than parliament, and authority rather than the rights of the individual.

Within a given country, tension is increased or decreased by the facts of the situation—the relationship between the size of the population and the total resources. According to their traditions, beliefs, and temperament, the masses are more or less prone to violent solutions but, in the last resort, the dominant factor is perhaps political rather than economic. The weakness, inefficiency, and contradictions of the ruling class aid and abet subversive movements. If the masses are under the impression that development is hamstrung by the social structure, they rush to extremes as soon as they emerge from their age-old passivity. It is wrong to suppose that the rate of growth determines the attitude of the masses, who are contented when the rate is high and unruly when it is low. On the contrary, rates of growth are only statistical averages and they are no guide to the obstreperous, passive, or resigned behavior of the populace and the various classes in any given country. What is certain on this level of generalization is that, now more than ever, corrupt and powerless oligarchies that fail to introduce reforms felt to be both economically necessary and morally imperative by the body of the nation are digging their own graves.

There is nothing surprising in this conclusion. The chief virtue of a Soviet regime, as far as growth is concerned, is political rather than economic. It establishes a strong authority at the summit and, by means of the single party, ensures the transmission of directives throughout the whole of society. When the existing regime is unable to govern or to transmit its orders, the Soviet pattern seems to offer a solution.

Perhaps we can go further and ask a similar question about the later phases of development. When a community has reached a certain stage of maturity, does it call for any particular regime, i.e., which regime is the most suitable and which is the most likely? These questions get us to the heart of the matter. If we agree that the creation or development of an industrial society is the aim of all peoples, is this aim definite enough in itself for us to conclude that all countries which reach a comparable stage of development tend to resemble each other? In other words, do the conflicts between the different kinds of regimes tend to die down as economic progress becomes marked?

One hears the most contradictory opinions about the present ideological situation. Some people maintain that we are involved in a struggle to the death between incompatible world views, and that what is at stake is the control of minds and the whole structure of the future. Others claim that ideologies are dying out and that all nations are gradually coming to understand not only that they are interdependent but also that their achievements and aspirations are similar. I shall formulate my own opinions under four headings:

1. On the social and economic level, all countries in all latitudes and whatever the racial origins of their inhabitants express the same aspirations, based on fundamentally similar values. The time is now long past when a marshal of France could preach a return to the land. No one would now dare to be hostile to industrialization and urbanization. There is no state or regime that does not proclaim its ambition to increase and improve its output and to ensure a less unfair distribution of the increased production resulting from the rise in productivity. This may, in some cases, be the homage that vice pays to virtue, but it may also be recognition of values now accepted as inevitable. At the same time, rascist doctrines are almost everywhere repudiated, in words if not in deeds, as if no one any longer dared deny the universal destiny of mankind.

It follows that the conflict between the Soviet and the Western systems, at least with regard to social and economic matters, arises less from differences about ends than from differences about means. The supporters of Sovietization claim that only revolution can ensure the full development of productive forces and equitable distribution of the fruits of development. They claim that the revolution can only be carried through by an all-powerful Communist Party. Lastly, they argue that only revolution can guarantee freedom, since, in the absence of revolution, men are condemned to exploitation and enslavement by the owners of the means of production and by monopolists. All these assertions are, in my view, groundless. The Soviet system, with its harsh methods and its abolition of all personal liberty, seems to me excusable only as a means, inevitable, perhaps, but in itself deplorable, of bringing about rapid modernization.

It is true that the conflict between the two halves of the world has a much greater significance on the religious level. The West is not, properly speaking, Christian, although it has a great many links with Christianity. On the other hand, it is not officially atheistic or hostile to religion. Western states, as a rule, are neutral toward the church or toward the faith of the individual; they are not armed with any religious conviction mixed with political truth. The Soviet state is different in that it is openly hostile to the churches and imposes—as an integral part of a political truth which is proclaimed to be the official, national truth—an ideology excluding all belief in the transcendent. In the long-term view, the real conflict between the Soviet Union and the West relates not so much to the methods of economic modernization as to men's rights to form their own conception of their destiny, over and above the building of steel and concrete pyramids.

2. In the Western countries, the ideological quarrels inherited from the nineteenth century or the beginning of the twentieth have by now lost their virulence. The intellectual debate continues about the extent to which planning should take precedence over market mechanisms or collective ownership of the means of production over private ownership, but even among professional economists only a few specialists are excited by the argument, and it seems to have lost all interest for the mass of the population. In Western Europe, the experience of the last fifteen years has shown that development is now the watchword of both the Right and the Left, and that even when it comes to sharing out the national income, the Left is not alone in desiring to reduce inequalities.

In a sense, it would not be wrong to define the advanced countries as those in which the Left and the Right are no longer opposed to each other on the question of development, because development can take place without any further fundamental changes. Some systems, professions, or undertakings may be adversely affected by expansion, but their representatives are just as likely to tend toward "Poujadism," which is considered a right-wing movement, as toward Communism, which is considered left-wing.

3. It is true to say that ideologies are dead in the advanced societies of the West, if we take an ideology to be a total interpretation of world history, but the statement does not apply to countries in process of development. They are in the grip of a controversy as passionate as it is confused.

Not only do they hesitate between the various patterns of development presented by the age, they also have a tendency to confuse the search for a method appropriate to their particular problems with the choice between the foreign patterns vaunted by rival propaganda systems. At the same time, the initial stage of economic development usually demands fairly radical social changes. It often happens that certain slogans, which at first sight seem left-wing in character, have a conservative significance. (This is the case, for instance, when representative institutions are dominated by plutocrats or big landowners.) There is a danger that political values relating to freedom may contradict, or seem to contradict, economic values connected with development.

4. How are East-West relations and the great ideological schism affected by the fact that the advanced countries tend toward ideological reconciliation, whereas the countries in process of development are still in the throes of ideological dispute? Can we say that the Soviet Union, through the effects of economic progress, is losing the intransigence of her revolu-

tionary youth? According to Khrushchev, President Kennedy's grandsons will find themselves living under a socialist system. We also know that, according to Kennedy, Premier Khrushchev's grandchildren will find themselves living in a free country, that is, under a regime of the Western type. If we have to decide between these two statements, I would opt—at the risk of being accused of wishful thinking—for the one which happens to coincide with my preferences. It seems to me that common sense and probability are on the Kennedy side. Why should a wealthy society such as the United States accept the rigors of Sovietization? For the supposition to take on even a vague likelihood, we have to imagine either an American military defeat or another great depression worse than the previous one. Assuming that such catastrophes do not occur, we can expect Russia to become more like America. As the revolution fades into the distance and the standard of living rises, the Soviet regime may have to allow more latitude to the wishes of the consumers, attach more importance to the economic nature of investments, and allow greater liberty to individuals and ideas.

But why should we decide between rival claims that cannot both be true and that may both be false? There are no grounds for believing that all advanced societies must be of the same type and that history must set its seal on the final victory of the Kremlin or the Capitol. Stalinism, in its extreme and even aberrant form, is not easily reconcilable with the needs of a highly rationalized, industrial society, but the single-party system and a state ideology are. Within a so-called Marxist framework, there is room for a great deal of ideological discussion, just as organized competition can exist within the context of the single party.

This being so, the main lesson to be drawn is in the nature of a counsel of wisdom rather than of a prophecy. Long after the world has been united by technology, men will continue to believe in rival gods. To survive, they must learn to live with their differences. This, of course, is the meaning of peaceful coexistence. But for coexistence to be genuinely peaceful, it must also be ideological. In other words, the believers must accept the principle of mutual tolerance. War, it is said, begins in men's souls. Peace transcending coexistence will begin when one side tolerates the rights and opinions of the other.

II

Development Theory and
Evolutionist Philosophy

PROFESSOR MORRIS GINSBERG * argues that
the "evolutionary" or "rational" interpretation of
the history of mankind has lost ground since the last
century. There is no justification for such skepticism,
and it is discounted by the scientific practice of those who deny
the theory that history develops according to a universal pat-

* In a report that is reprinted in Bert Hoselitz and Wilbert Moore, eds.,
Industrialization and Society (New York: Humanities Press, 1965).

tern. "Growth" and "development" are terms used by historians and scientists, but they have no meaning unless they are related to value judgments which are better stated explicitly. Moreover, "if the process of development is to be controlled, it is necessary to have fuller knowledge not only of the factors involved in social change but also of the goals or ends toward which change is to be directed."

In his search for a theory of social development that is valid for all mankind and for society as a whole, Professor Ginsberg discovers criteria which would have been acceptable to sociologists of the last century; one of the features of human history is the progressive application of reason and morals. His conclusion is worth quoting: "On the whole, it seems to me, the evidence is strongly in favor of the growing importance of the moral factor in the shaping of social life. . . . The growth of legality in the history of mankind and the unification of legal systems, overriding political boundaries, affords impressive evidence of the totality of the efforts toward a rational ordering of human relations, and in this, as we have seen, moral factors play an important role."

It is not my intention to argue about Professor Ginsberg's thesis. What I should like to make clear is the reason why the historical consciousness of our contemporaries does not easily accept this "global," rational, humanitarian conception of development, although it is consonant with the ideas of the earliest sociologists. Why, in other words, when we attempt to make the transition from the economic theory of development, which is held by every school of thought (albeit in different forms), to a theory of the development of society as a whole and of mankind, difficulties arise which many people think insuperable and which are apparently either ignored or underestimated in Professor Ginsberg's report?

I

Whether consciously or not, sociologists and economists obviously hold some sort of theory of development, for they have no hesitation or reservations about speaking of underdeveloped countries and of the moral, political, and social need for promoting or hastening their development. I shall, therefore, first attempt to define the theory of development implicit in the concepts used by economists.

One way of doing this—the simplest way—is to take the various criteria of *under*development that have been used by writers, and from their opposites deduce the criteria of development.

In an underdeveloped country, the national level of production is typically low, and the per-capita income is therefore small. It is possible that because the peasants in underdeveloped countries are self-supporting and price systems are radically different from those in highly developed countries, the evaluation of the national per-capita income is distorted. If, however, we conclude that computation of the national product in underdeveloped countries is invalid, the very inference would have a meaning. It would point to the difference in kind between economies in which most economic operations are expressed in monetary values and those in which most people are governed by custom and live close to the minimum subsistence level.

In any case, the volume of the national product or the per-capita income of the population is not a cause but an effect—or, rather, it is a statistic that reveals the form of activity of a given community. If the individual's income is low, the reason is that the work of the population as a whole is not very productive. And in turn, the low level of production is related to the distribution of the total labor force among each sector (primary, secondary, and tertiary). The productivity of labor can hardly be low if a high percentage of the labor force is engaged in industry. It follows that in underdeveloped countries the majority of the population is engaged in agriculture and is therefore rural; as a rule, industrialization and urbanization go hand in hand. If the bulk of the population lives in villages and the state's resources are small, school attendance will be low and the illiteracy rate high. Furthermore, both the birth rate and the death rate will be comparatively high. But because health measures are not very costly today and are very effective, the death rate in most cases falls more rapidly than the birth rate, and underdeveloped countries have a comparatively high rate of population growth.

One point should be made clear from the beginning. The notion of underdevelopment has its origin in a comparison; it refers to what societies are *not* (i.e., highly developed) and does not refer positively to what they are. The concept of underdevelopment (or of inadequate development) is applied to ancient civilizations, such as India, tribal civilizations, such as in certain parts of Africa, as well as to the poorer areas of highly developed countries. One may even say that it is unreasonable to try to give a positive, clear-cut definition of underdevelopment since it is essentially a comparative concept. The factors found in every case of underdevelopment are those which are intrinsically linked to a low rate of labor productivity*—i.e., a predominance of agricultural labor and traditional

* It is possible to imagine a comparatively high rate of per-capita income in an unindustrialized country where the population is small and land plentiful. This is or was the case in some Latin American countries, such as Argentina.

modes of tillage, the lack or inadequacy of industry, etc. There are even degrees of variation within these structural features of underdevelopment. We still speak of some countries with a high rate of industrial production in absolute terms as under-developed. In many of these countries a modern sector of the population exists side by side with a traditional sector. The margin of variation is much wider still if the criteria used are demographic and social instead of economic. In some of the underdeveloped countries of Africa, the birth rate was until recently—and in some cases still is—excessively low, and the population is threatened with extinction. The relationship be-tween the number of people and the country's resources is not necessarily very unfavorable; everything depends on the dis-tribution of the population with respect to its size; in some places the relationship is better than in others. The concept of underdevelopment, in short, came into being by analogy with industrial societies, and its value is limited. It would be more useful to classify the varieties of underdevelopment ac-cording to the social type to which the population belongs, the relative size of the modernized section, and the way in which modern ideas have spread.

We can, however, draw one conclusion from this brief anal-ysis which will help us in our study of the theory of develop-ment. What economists (and even sociologists) now call de-velopment or growth is the establishment of an economy in which labor is productive and where the over-all national or per-capita output is large. Such an economy is essentially a progressive one; once an economy has been modernized its national production rate can be expected to rise annually. Because statisticians use the same methods for underdeveloped countries and developed countries and can trace the growth of *both* types of country and also the progress of a country from one stage to the other, people receive the impression that the difference between the two is merely one of degree. This is, of course, incorrect; progressiveness is the hallmark of a modern economy, which is alive to results, repudiates tradition, and is willing to change its habits so as to produce more in less time and to produce different goods by using new methods.

The contrast between development and underdevelopment is qualitative and not quantitative, although it can be expressed in figures. It illustrates the difference between two attitudes toward nature and work, two forms of organization, perhaps two ages in human history. Instead of seeking a coherent and complete definition of underdevelopment—which is obviously impossible, since it is a negative concept—let us consider what development is or, to put it another way, what conception of development is implicit in scientific practice and theory today.

Our initial approach should be the same as in the case of underdevelopment. Statisticians and economists call a country developed if the per-capita income of the population is above a certain sum (e.g., $800 per annum). Such a sum is attainable only if a certain proportion of the labor force is engaged in industry* and if industrial work is itself productive. If industrial work is to be productive, however, managers, engineers, and trained staff are needed, and technical training is necessary from the lowest ranks to the highest. Within certain limits, industrialization, urbanization, and education go hand in hand.

These social criteria, however, are superficial. It is true that in societies that are called developed a large proportion of the population lives in the towns, the literacy rate is high, and a

---

* Except in a few cases where the population is very small in relation to the land available and the income high because agriculture is rationalized.

large proportion of the labor force is engaged in industry; it is also true that such societies are progressive and aim at raising the national production rate and the per-capita income every year, that the birth rate is in most cases lower than in the past or than in contemporary underdeveloped countries, that the mortality rate—particularly the infant mortality rate—is always low (the standards of social health and mass education guarantee a falling mortality rate). These are all facts which in themselves cannot be questioned, but they do not quite satisfy the sociologist or economist who wants to get behind these observations and grasp the basic reason why certain societies are developed, or the distinctive feature of such societies.

Personally, I think we are justified in considering the application of the scientific mentality to production as the ultimate cause and at the same time the essence of development. To think in terms of productivity or output is in a certain sense to ask the question which is characteristic of the scientific mind—that is, the analytical, quantitative mind: How can the same results be obtained with less land or less labor? How can production be raised with the same amount of work or the same amount of land? How can more commodities be manufactured in the same time? To calculate input and output, the productivity of the soil and of labor, time and production, is characteristic of the spirit from which science springs and which science propagates in turn.

At the same time, science provides the means by which problems of this type may be solved—tools and machinery. It endows each worker with an increasing store of mechanical energy beyond the dreams of our forebears. Besides lightening man's toil in the mine and in the field by substituting the tool for the hand, science invents technological instruments to meet man's needs, both eternal and elementary, to an extent never believed possible. Technological inventions, such as radio, television, and motorcars, are in fact means of transportation and communication that, though they create the particular form of the need, do not create the needs themselves, which are as old as the human race.

All technological inventions, which economists call either investment goods or durable consumer goods, belong to one of three types—they may be sources of power, they may be tools, or they may fulfill man's eternal needs, henceforth amplified in various forms.* Perhaps the first two types could be combined, since machinery often includes both the tool and the system of movement and control it requires. A recent development, the importance of which is often not recognized, is the progress made in the production of household implements. The vacuum cleaner, the refrigerator, and the washing machine lighten women's work as the pneumatic drill lightens the miner's.

It seems to me that productivity and mechanization (in the widest sense) are both expressions of the scientific spirit, and both are essential to development. It would be impracticable to transfer manpower to industry if agriculture were not capable of feeding the same number of mouths while employing fewer men. Granted that the agrarian population in traditional society was too large and that industry is now employing labor which formerly produced nothing, it is still essential that industry be able to find work for hands that were once idle. Thus we have an unending dialectic between producing the same

---

* We have taken the motorcar and television as examples because of the evident specificity of the desire for these. The analysis would be easier and clearer if applied to housing or clothing.

things better and in larger quantities and producing different things—between producing goods of the same kind in a different way and producing goods which had never been thought of before. The exact form that the satisfaction of an aspiration takes is the result of scientific progress, but the basic needs remain the same.

The typical economy of developed societies may properly be called *industrial*. Industry, indeed, is essential in order to absorb the manpower released as a result of increased agricultural productivity and in order to supply working tools and technical equipment. The tertiary sector yields a higher rate of individual income, but it is in part the by-product of the secondary, its social apparatus. The expansion of the tertiary sector is made possible by the primary and secondary sectors; a high rate of agricultural and industrial production justifies the transfer of large numbers of workers to administration or to recreation and leisure activities. At first glance, industry is, from the social point of view, the hallmark of the developed society.

The introduction of machinery or factories, however, does not of itself ensure the development of a society. The entire social apparatus, the social structures, which are the expression of industry and are essential to it, must be transplanted. A society is not truly industrialized until the actions of men and the operation of institutions are in harmony with the spirit of industry. Provisionally, we have called the spirit of modern economy scientific. Fundamentally, industrialized societies may be called scientific, in that both mechanization and productivity are the fruit of the scientific spirit and are the ultimate causes of both industrialization and the progressive nature of the economy.

II

The concept of industrial or scientific society at which we have arrived by analyzing underdevelopment and development raises in its turn objections and criticisms. As I see it, in the final analysis, there are really only two.

Our definition of industrial or scientific society has been based on features common to both the Soviet and the Western systems. In the sort of statistical survey of which Clark's *Conditions of Economic Progress* is the protoype and pattern, all countries can be examined, whether they have a planned economy or not and whether their leaders profess allegiance to Marx or Keynes, history or God. Furthermore, all countries, even those whose systems of government are opposed, may be placed in order according to the same criterion, the first being the one that has the highest per-capita income. For similar reasons, which are opposite in their implications, convinced Communists and anti-Communists alike reject development theory that groups together societies basically foreign and hostile to each other; they dismiss as artificial the comparison of systems that are determined to destroy each other.

This first criticism—that Soviet and Western societies should not be seen as two species within the same genus or type—presupposes another: that criteria adopted for the definition of development are inadequate for defining a social order. Just as there are many kinds of development, so there are, and will be in the future, many kinds of underdevelopment. The one concept is no better than the other; both should be rejected at the same time.

In a certain sense, this second criticism is unanswerable. A group cannot be defined in concrete terms by the criterion of development. Industry may be either privately or publicly owned. The resources of the group are allocated to various tasks either by decision of a planning bureau or as a result of the innumerable decisions made by individuals who have no precise knowledge of the consequences of their decisions. In the one case, the division of the national income between investment and savings is the conscious objective of a plan which is itself consciously worked out by a bureau, while in the other case it is the consequence—generally, the fortuitous consequence—of the acts of many separate individuals. (The two systems, of course, never occur in a pure form and in practice are more or less mixed.)

In other words, the economy of an industrial society inevitably belongs to one system or the other. This does not mean that the concept is not legitimate. The Greek city-state was a type of society, and the various city-states had certain characteristics in common: the size of the group, the citizenship of fighting men, the use of slave labor, the distinction between citizens and aliens, etc. Similarly, all societies that obey scientific laws in organizing production have characteristics in common. It remains to be discovered, however, which are the common characteristics and which represent a choice between different forms.

A detailed discussion of the distinction I have just indicated between the genus and the species of an industrial society would be outside the scope of this short study. I shall give only a few examples of the kind of analysis that is needed.

I have said that the application of the scientific spirit to the organization of production is of the essence of an industrial society. One may, I think, infer from this that every industrial society tends to raise production and productivity to a maximum either one after the other or simultaneously; that it sees itself in the process of historical development, because growth appears to it consonant with its true order of being; and that it is, therefore, animated by the spirit of quantity and progress. In the long run, indifference to the amount of wealth and to the future is incompatible with the spirit of modern science as applied to production; even if we reject science's latest creations, how can we refuse to produce the same goods at lower cost and smaller outlay?

Is the stress on the pre-eminence of the group as opposed to the welfare of the individual so basic that it distinguishes between two types of scientific society, according to the objectives defined by their leaders? I do not think so. I believe that at any moment in history a society in the course of development may assign a larger or smaller percentage of its resources to consumption. In this sense, we may say, symbolically, that one group gives more to the living and the other to future generations. Hitherto, however, no highly developed society has denied that affluence is its final objective, whatever immediate concern it may have shown with the exigencies of power. Only when war appears to be inevitable can industrial societies reasonably subordinate individual welfare to collective strength as a matter of principle.

On the other hand, the experience of history shows that it is impossible to deduce the ownership of the means of production from a knowledge of the chief characteristics of a given industrial society. A business must be run with an eye on output—the object must be to produce; it is possible to imagine managers who are appointed by the state or by administrative boards and who inherit their position of authority, although inheritance of administrative positions seems to be gradually dying out.

The distinction between public and private ownership differs essentially from the distinction between individual welfare and group pre-eminence. The first conceals the uncertain legal status of business firms and of their relation with the state in respect of the main features of industrial society. In practice, however, an industrial society always adopts one or other of the two alternatives. If we imagine the whole of mankind united in one universal state, there will still be two possible types of ownership. But the choice between individual welfare and group pre-eminence would have no meaning in a universal state. It is bound up with the plurality of states in violent conflict. The proportion of investment to consumption would, of course, continue to vary with the rate of expansion desired: the greater the rate of expansion, the higher must be the rate of investment and the lower the rate of consumption. The choice between present and future sometimes occurs in combination with the choice between individual and collective welfare, since the same groups uphold the primacy of expansion and of the future. The primacy of expansion, however (or rather, of a high rate of expansion), does not mean that the goal is not abundance. The object of every industrial society is to assert the power of man over nature (of which the power of some men over others is an unavoidable consequence), as well as to increase the output of goods or merchandise.

It seems to me that the abstract conception of industrial society as a type can be shown to be legitimate both by comparison with pre-industrial societies and in view of the consequences to which the basic characteristics of the type inevitably lead. Every historical grouping had been based on the peasantry, which constituted the majority of the population; in industrial societies, the labor force engaged in cultivation of the soil can be reduced to less than 10 per cent of the whole. All historical groups, whether political units or classes, had relied on force, conquest, and plunder to gain their share of a supposedly fixed store of wealth; from now on, they are all able to increase their wealth without reducing that of others. The very essence of the industrial society implies marked changes in two aspects of collective living—housing and working conditions on the one hand, and war on the other.

Now it is possible to see why the concept of development is more useful and less open to criticism than that of underdevelopment. Societies that have insufficiently applied the scientific spirit are underdeveloped. But at the same time, they are as highly diversified as the societies of the past. Underdeveloped countries display not only a multiplicity of surviving historical forms but also the diversity due to the differing ways that each group experiences the effects of progress. On the other hand, development includes and implies the structural characteristics of the type of society we have called industrial.

Does this mean that those on both the right and the left who emphasize the differences between the Soviet system and the capitalist (or Western) system are wrong? Not necessarily. Athens and Sparta were both city-states; they belonged to the same type of society and could understand each other's point of view, but at the same time they were prone to contention, since the values embodied in one were—or seemed to be—denied by the other. Industrial societies are by no means all alike; they differ in their economic systems, social relations, political forms, and scales of values. The characteristics com-

mon to both Soviet and Western forms perhaps matter less to
the people (or the leaders) of both than their differences and
incompatibilities. We may at least say, provisionally, that the
concept of development or of industrial society does not as yet
answer the question whether the social organization of such
societies is, or will be, the same.

The ideological aspect of the discussion now falls into two
parts. Some people—both Marxists and non-Marxists—declare that Soviet and Western societies will inevitably grow
more and more alike, since their forces of production will become increasingly similar. On this point—to what extent will
similarity of productive forces imply similarity of social organization?—scientists and politicians take opposite sides. Both in
the East and in the West, the former gives an affirmative and
the latter a negative reply. The second issue concerns the stages
of development, which is another way of speculating about the
characteristics of this society that is declared to be the same in
any latitude and under any form of government.

Let us begin with the second issue, the *schedule of development*. In the Soviet Union, the official Marxist view is that
there is a succession of systems (set forth by Marx in the preface to *A Contribution to the Critique of Political Economy*)—
the economy of ancient times, based on slaves; the medieval
economy, based on serfs; the capitalist economy, based on
wage earners; and the socialist economy of the future, in which
man will no longer exploit his fellows. (Asian systems of
production, which Marx put aside and did not treat as a
stage in Western development, are usually omitted.) This
scheme presupposes that each regime in the history of mankind is determined by the relations of man to work or by the
legal status of the manual worker (slave, serf, or wage

earner). It also presupposes that in a highly developed society the relations between the partners in production may be basically different from what is known as wage-earning relationships.

An example of the Western answer to the Marxist position is that given by W. W. Rostow. It is based on two ideas: that there is a difference in kind between traditional societies and modern or industrial societies; and that the difference between the various stages of development (in the industrial age) lies in the level of production reached and the per-capita income. Hence, there are five generally accepted phases: the traditional society, the transitional society (in which the stage is set for change), the society which is in the crucial, early stages of progress, the society which is approaching maturity (when the new production methods become general throughout the entire economy), and, lastly, the society of mass consumption.

In many respects, this theory of phases of development is more questionable than the theory of industrial society. In taking traditional society as its starting point, it is in danger of making the mistake (indeed, it seems to make it) which is inherent in the concept of underdevelopment—that is, it places in one category all societies which are not developed. The second phase—the transitional one—is also questionable on the grounds that its various historical forms are an extension of those of the first phase, and that the essential differences within this period are due to variations in the nature of traditional society and to its encounter with developed societies. There is a danger (which Rostow does not deny) that this scheme may conceal the tremendous differences between independent development (as in Europe and the United States) and development brought on from outside or development through imitation. Development varies with the scientific or technical stage reached. Great Britain passed through the first three stages very quickly, but did not reach the fourth, and certainly not the fifth, until after World War II, which shows that development is not automatic (a fact Rostow does not attempt to deny), but that its rate of progress is governed by numerous factors, and that the more or less even progress indicated by national production statistics or percapita income figures gives a false idea of the complex and sometimes dramatic nature of development.

We shall consider only the main points at issue in this problem: Is the capitalist economy, considered as a stage in the history of mankind, adequately defined by the wage system? And if modernity is essentially the scientific or industrial spirit, can capitalism and the Soviet system legitimately be regarded as necessary stages of evolution? Not only do I reply to both these questions in the negative, but I defy any economist or sociologist who is sincere and not answerable to the state to reply in the affirmative.

It would, of course, be foolish to deny that the wage system was characteristic of capitalist economies and still is so in the twentieth century (providing a reasonably wide interpretation is given to the term "wage system"). But the marked increase in the means of production and the radical changes in working and living conditions (which Marx observed and for which he gave credit to the bourgeoisie) that historically accompanied the wage system have no essential connection with it, nor could they be inferred from the actual notion of capitalism or wage earning. Through the experience of the Soviet countries, it is now known that the development of the forces of production, which Marx regarded as capitalism's historic mission, can be achieved through the efforts of the state or of a party or a class of aristocratic origin, as well as through the work of private enterprise. We know that centralized planning is as favorable to development as is a market economy. It is obviously illogical to take an organizational feature, wage earning,* as characterizing a historical phase rather than the criterion of the development of productive forces, which is common to all industrializing societies, although lacking in societies that have the wage system yet are not being modernized.

Therefore, as regards Marx's scheme, we are obliged by the facts of history at least to admit that the order in which systems succeed each other is not the same as the order of the successive stages of growth (the determinative element being taken as the amount of per-capita income). At each stage of development (in Clark's sense), we have seen that there are both planned systems and market economies, although, despite the difference between the systems, some similar or identical phenomena were to be found in each.

Does this mean that the Soviet thesis (that all industrial societies will eventually become socialist) or the thesis of some Western thinkers (that Soviet societies, as they develop, will tend to approximate the Western type) are indefensible and do not accord with the facts? Certainly not. It may be maintained that some features of both Soviet and Western societies can be expected to spread throughout the world, but in the present state of our historical experience and our conceptual analyses, these features are not so simple or so easy to discern as a planned or market economy or public or private

---

* It should be added that the wage system, strictly speaking, exists in the Soviet Union as well as in the West—unless it is stipulated that wages imply private ownership of the means of production.

ownership. For the time being, we shall simply note the two conclusions we have reached: that all industrial societies may become more and more alike, but that it would appear that this universal society will not be obliged to make a definite choice between a planned economy and a market economy or between public and private ownership.

III

The scientific society is far from being universal, but it is potentially so, in the sense that it has now become a *sine qua non* of power and prosperity. Nations that deliberately reject scientific development are choosing to leave the path of history and to stagnate. They would appear doomed, unwittingly, to final annihilation.

If, then, a particular type of society appears to be destined to permeate all civilizations, if all races are willing to adopt the same principles of conduct, work, and organization, why is the evolutionary conception of history not more generally accepted? The use we make of concepts of development and underdevelopment shows that the image of the future in which we implicitly believe is no different from that inherent in the great doctines of the last century—that the end of all histories is *one* history, that all societies will ultimately become *one* society and embody the same basic principles. Why has the economic-sociological theory of development not led to a revival of evolutionist philosophies?

There are, I think, a number of answers to this question, and we shall examine them one by one. The first stresses the difference between the concepts used in the past and those we use today. Is the content of the phrases "development" and "industrial society," or "scientific society," the same—have they the same overtones—as "rationalization" or "moralization"? Industrialization is inevitable, its tendency is to become generalized. Is it the same thing as rationalization?

We must define our terms, particularly the word "rational." Behavior that cannot but be called rational may seem from another point of view as irrational. It is rational to provide ourselves with the weapons needed to overcome our enemy, but is it rational that belligerents generally should use phosphorus bombs to burn cities or atomic bombs to kill millions of people at once? In other words, unquestioned rationality is strictly a means, and for the moment we shall set aside the problem of the ends toward which the rationality of means is directed.

With this reservation, it can hardly be denied that mankind today is applying scientific knowledge more than ever and that scientific knowledge is greater and more exact than ever before. And, what is more, scientific knowledge is advancing more and more rapidly—if for no other reason than the rapid increase in the number of scientists.

However we define rationality, it seems evident that the natural sciences are the product of reason. Accuracy of concepts, sound reasoning, ever greater refinement of ideas, the relating of fields that appear unrelated, the tendency to systematize results while being willing to re-evaluate and adopt new basic hypotheses or principles—all these are typical of what we, in our day, understand by "reason." We might even go further and say that today we define reason through science rather than science through reason, simply because science is a reality we can apprehend whereas reason (if it is anything more than the ability to think scientifically) is a debatable concept.

Another point that needs to be explained is the rapid scientific progress made since the sixteenth century and especially in the twentieth century. Nobody thinks that the Greeks, the Chinese, or the Indians had a different sort of reasoning faculty from that of modern man or that they had none at all. Yet the decisive step, beyond which the accumulation of knowledge seems almost certain, was taken only a few centuries ago, in one particular sector of civilization. We shall not venture even to put forward a theory as to this particular achievement of the Western world in the modern age, but it may be said that the progress of natural science and the increasing wealth of scientific research have more to them than sound reasoning, the definition of concepts, the systematization of results, and the critical faculty. Scientific progress depends on the establishment of a certain relation between abstract thought and experience, and this relation, in turn, can only be established by a particular type of reasoning—one that prefers quantifiable propositions and requires explanations to be subject to confirmation or refutation by facts. Perhaps Lévy-Bruhl was wrong in thinking that the mind of primitive man differed from that of civilized man. It is not so much that the reasoning faculty of primitive minds is different from ours, but rather that their basic hypotheses, their metaphysics, are different. It is probable that thinkers today are, even superficially, more rational than their predecessors—I mean, that their reasoning is sounder and their concepts more clearly defined. This, however, is not the heart of the matter. They are better because they combine abstract thought and experience, because of their method of interrogating nature and taking it for granted that intelligibility should have a particular philosophical essence. In short, rationality in science is connected with methodology in the widest sense of the term. Methodology, however, is bound up with what we may call a philosophical conception of the truth, both methodology and conception being confirmed by success.

Similarly, we must admit that technology and industry are rational. Man has always had to obtain a livelihood by engaging in some activity—by work. His work has been more or less effective, it has included the transformation of natural resources and the creation of a regular supply of resources through the use of biological phenomena, and it has given man greater mastery over his environment—or at least a growing independence of it. Auguste Comte's words need no repeating—"The way from knowledge to power is a direct road." The rationality of knowledge makes for greater power. As a means, increased power is by definition increased rationality. Leaving aside for the moment the direct and indirect consequences of technological progress, whether in agriculture or in industry, we see that progress itself marks the development of practical rationality, just as the accumulation of knowledge indicates the development of theoretical rationality.

From technical rationality as manifested in science and production, there is a logical transition to the rationality of social organization, or at least of some of its aspects. Is it not rational to increase the collective output by sharing the tasks to be done? And is not this division of labor essentially the same thing as combining physical resources, materials, or tools? Law and administration, too, are becoming rational in certain senses of the word.

The rationalization of the legal system implies that definitions of concepts, and consequently of what is permitted and what forbidden, shall be as exact as possible, that reasoning as to the conclusions to be drawn from concepts shall be as sound as possible, both in doctrine and in jurisprudence, and that systematization shall be as complete as possible. On this point, however, the tendency is not so clearly marked as in science and technology. Scientific or technical rationality is not commensurate with juridical rationality as it has just been described. Collective ownership and the primacy of the public interest over individual rights entail a decline of juridical rationality compared with the societies of nineteenth-century Europe. Even in the West, because of changes in economic systems and social ideas, the law is perhaps less consistent than it was half a century ago, its principles less uniform, and the reasoning of legal doctrine or of the courts less unchallengeable.

Law in any scientific society, when compared with law in primitive societies or those which are not secularized or differentiated, is more rational—that is, it is abstract, its concepts are well defined, and its reasoning is sound. But without closer examination, we are not justified in saying that law is evolving in the direction of ever greater rationalization. Whether the law is relatively consistent or inconsistent, whether it is more or less predictable, whether its principles are more or less clear and its applications of those principles more or less consistently deduced—all this depends on whether the social order is changing or temporarily stabilized and on the aspect of the individual's life or of the state with which society is most concerned.

As for administration, it appears at first sight to be growing more and more complex. Social insurance and tax laws cover an ever wider field and require more and more officials. These types of administration are more rational in the sense that laws and regulations aim at covering a larger number of cases, at defining principles applicable to a larger number of human situations, and at determining both the exact rights and the exact obligations of individuals despite the endless variety of activities in which they engage. The more attempts are made to match regulations to the infinite wealth of actuality, the more failures or near failures there are. Rationality is unquestionably making progress, though primarily as a goal; and it is in view of the scale of these goals that the results obtained (although in some respects less satisfactory than in former societies in which regulations covered less of human life) are held—rightly, in my opinion—to indicate increased rationality.

Production and the organization of the techniques and services needed in production are more rational than ever before. But what are the social and human consequences of this rationalization, the counterparts of which are the effort to produce at all costs and the uncontrollable impetus of technological invention? Or, to put it in another way, is a society reasonable if its prime object is to produce as much as possible?

IV

The problem that issues from the foregoing analyses might be stated in the most general terms as follows: From the philosophic point of view, is the progress of scientific, technological, and administrative rationality real progress?

Some people will say that the question in itself is meaningless, that progress can be assessed only by reference to values, and, as value judgments are not subject to proof and reflect subjective preferences, what is the use of discussing the question? The decision whether there is progress or not depends on individual preferences.

I do not think this objection is valid. Even if we accept this negation of philosophy, it is a fact that in every age most people belonging to the same society or the same civilization reach approximate agreement about what is desirable. If the opponents of science and technology were the only people to question the value of rationalization, the discussion would have little significance.

Others will say that the world is losing its magic and that the sense of mystery and the ability to commune with nature are vanishing. It may be true that positivist science tends to destroy the religious faith of many. But the alternative is clear: either faith is incompatible with positivist science—and in that case the gradual elimination of superstition in our scale of values cannot be regretted; or, as I believe, it is only debased forms of religious belief that are affected, and in that case, too, the progress of scientific knowledge as such is the progress of mankind. How can we maintain that it is better to remain in ignorance than to know, better to believe what is not true than to demonstrate the truth?

What is problematical about scientific and technical progress is not progress itself but its consequences—the kind of society it is likely to bring into being and the condition of man in that society. What strikes one is not so much the objections of reactionaries and romantics—people who have always had a horror of machines, quantity, and masses—as the questioning of history by "progressives" themselves.

By and large, it may be said that pessimistic interpretations of the industrial society issue from three schools, symbolized in the three names of Aldous Huxley, George Orwell, and Oswald Spengler.

The first of these schools distrusts the *brave new world*—it is afraid of boredom and comfort, the mediocrity and spiritual impoverishment of a universal lower middle class equipped with the latest technical gadgets. The second school consists of Western thinkers who see the final pathological form of Stalinism as prophetic of mankind's future; through technology, it is possible not only to change the nature of material things but also to juggle with man's conscience, not only to stop armed conflict but also to keep the world in a permanent state of war. In a technological age, total tyranny would become possible for the first time, since the conscience itself would no longer be invulnerable. The third school differs from the first two in that Spengler denies the basic originality of our society. Consequently, he regards urbanization, the reign of money and the masses—the phase which he calls civilization—as the stage immediately before the end of a "culture," the return to chaos which precedes a new upheaval. The three pessimistic forecasts are, then, a universal lower middle class, total tyranny, and the decline of the West.

Our Soviet colleagues will retort that there are no such pessimists in socialist countries, that such pessimism is typical of systems which have lost confidence in themselves and are mistaking their own collapse for the decline of the human race. It is perfectly true that pessimists of this sort can only be found in those Western countries in which the people's view of history is not dictated by state decrees. When the philosophy of development is an integral part of the official credo, heresies are by definition impossible.

We may agree at once to disregard the first of the three schools mentioned. Not that the question raised in it is meaningless—on the contrary, the problem raised by the portrayal of a society which has become scientific and which controls even personal relations, love and reproduction, is a very real one. Stated in abstract terms, the question asked is, "How will man live, once childish quarrels lose their point, illusions vanish, and the power of science is increased?" But we are not in a position to answer this question because we know nothing about it. We are neither able nor willing to arrest the march of science on the ground that man may be incapable of making proper use of it, or to perpetuate unhappiness because happiness may stultify men. In any case, we are not likely to see a world without tragedies, wars, and unhappiness in the near future.

Let us also dismiss Spengler's pessimism. Even if we accept his ideas about the plurality of "cultures" and the ultimate, incommunicable originality of each, two facts can be asserted in relation to our own times, one of which is without precedent and the other at least quantitatively new. Contact, communication, and conflict among many cultures are now the rule. A universal society is coming into being. The achievements of science and technology are now on such a scale that it is becoming impossible to base our ideas of what the future will be like on what we know of the past. The West is dying as a separate "culture," but it has a future as the center of a universal society. It has lost its position as leader; it may retain its prosperity and creative energy.

There remains the second school of pessimism—the pessimism of *1984,* which may be expressed as follows: Why should technical media not be used in the service of tyranny and war? Or, to put it still more abstractly, the rationalization of the means of production, of the administrative or juridical services, and of the economic system does not imply that power will be rightfully used, still less that it will be used to humanitarian ends.

The leaders of the Third Reich used a completely rationalized technical and bureaucratic administration to convey millions of human beings to the gas chambers and to exterminate them with maximum efficiency. If we assume that rationalization leads to moral conduct without explaining the systematic mass murders of the Third Reich, we must be singularly blind. The transport of the Jews was organized just as rationally as traffic in Paris or New York. In the death camps, books were kept as rationally as the books kept in youth camps. In short, to the extent that scientific, technical, economic, or administrative rationality is only a means, it can be used for any end— productive or destructive, hospitals or concentration camps, well-being or power, the unification or the extermination of mankind.

It will perhaps be said that the leaders of the Third Reich were madmen and monsters. That may be so, but at the same time it must be realized that in certain circumstances a highly cultured nation may select monsters and madmen as its leaders. There is a lesson to be learned from Khrushchev's speech at the Twentieth Congress. Even in a legitimate cause (such as agrarian collectivization), a leader corrupted by the "cult of personality" may employ methods that will lead to the death or deportation of millions. Social rationalization by force, even where the force is rationalized, sometimes leads to inhuman excesses.

It may be argued that scientific, technical, administrative, and economic rationalization not only is a means but implies a spiritual attitude, a social behavior profoundly opposed to the cruelties so common in our day. Here, indeed, is the core of the argument: Is the rationality of modern societies more than a means? Does it imply—must it logically imply—the application of moral principles to societies, a trend toward respect for humanitarian values? Modern science is the product of an attitude of mind that is rational in its ends, and not only in its means—regard for facts, sound reasoning, trust in other scientists, a critical attitude toward oneself and toward evidence. The scientist as scientist lives according to the dictates of reason. Does he as a man also live so? Does he consider the scientific attitude either possible for him or incumbent upon him outside the sphere of his search for truth?

Questions such as these have often been asked, and it is not easy to give categorical answers. To carry over the scientific virtues—prudence, humility, and deference to fact—into the field of action is praiseworthy; it is as though the transfer were induced by a sort of psychological contagion. But it is dictated purely by philosophical considerations, which most scientists do not consider as valid or as binding as the scientific establishment of facts and laws. Personally, I agree that there is no logical or scientific connection between science and a scientific attitude in other fields. One can only move from the one to the other by a realization of the human ideal implied in scientific research, and that realization is philosophical.

On the social plane, there is a twofold problem: (1) Is the individual changed by his absorption into a rational apparatus, whether technical or bureaucratic? (2) Are political or moral institutions becoming more and more rational under the influence of scientific and technical rationality?

The first of these problems appears the simpler. The individual acts in accordance with a certain rationality in the production chain or in the bureaucracy, but so long as he does not understand the organization as a whole and its purpose there is no reason why he should become any different—that he should become rational—outside his particular sphere of activity. Rational work performed without understanding does not change the human being as a whole. It does, of course, imply a minimum of education, but that is not enough to change the whole person. Moreover, even if the individual understands the organization as a whole, although he may perhaps become rational insofar as his intelligence permits, in fact this is not always the case.

Yet scientific and technical rationalization is not without its influence on the complex of moral ideas. Modern science in itself, in fact, admits of a virtual universality. It claims to be intelligible to all who accept its hard apprenticeship; it observes no frontiers between races or peoples. The community of scientists is a community of men as men, aside from social groups and their demands. Similarly, in a technical organization or a juridical system to which abstract conceptions have been applied, individuals are at the outset placed of necessity on the same footing. Their individual differences no longer matter—all that matters is their place in a relationship (e.g., creditor-debtor) or in an organization (official, wage earner, etc.). In this sense, rationalization today tends to gain acceptance for a universalist conception of morals.

Professor Ginsberg stresses this conception and considers that it is an advance; yet it is only an ideal, which is imperfectly realized in some groups. Precisely because it is more exacting, more ambitious, it is further from being practiced than were the ideas behind social orders in the past, which did not deny in law inequalities that existed in fact.

A distinction must be made between progress in ideals and progress in deeds. Scientific rationality tends to set up the idea of a universal society of all mankind. The twentieth-century ideal is loftier than that of any of the closed societies of the past which countenanced moral barriers between races and between peoples. At the same time, the clash between what should be and what is seems more violent in our day than in any other. If the virtue of man is to be measured by his loyalty to the values he professes, then our era is the most contemptible of all. In the past history of Europe, there is not one episode comparable to the industrial extermination of six million Jews.

Is it true to say that events of this sort are nonrecurring, that they are typical of a transitional stage in which attitudes surviving from the past combine with the promise and force of rationality to form an explosive mixture? In interpreting sociology and forecasting history, can we safely say that government and social customs will become more moral as a result of scientific and technical rationality?

In the present state of our experience, moral and humanitarian progress, whether in political institutions or in the individual way of life, does not seem to me to be a necessary result of rationality. Sociologists of the last century could not agree on the nature of the political system that would prevail in the industrial society. At present, we are apt to think that in the scientific age every system will be based on democratic watchwords, that all statesmen will govern in the name of the governed, in the name of the people, the proletariat, the race, and man's historic mission. It has been proved, however, that these watchwords do not exclude the possibility of even the worst features of tyranny. The alternative stated by Tocqueville a century ago—that a democratic society must be either despotic or liberal—seems to be more in line with our experience than any theory according to which the economic-social infrastructure results inevitably in one particular political system and only one.

So, above the conflict that rages between systems and ideologies, philosophers and sociologists ponder the question of the purpose of technical and administrative rationality. We should not listen to the pessimists who condemn the age as an age of robots, or to simpletons who think that physical comfort will result in increased good will and even produce more geniuses. We need only point to the obvious fact that neither production nor consumption is an end in itself. Complete satisfaction of basic needs (food, housing, clothing), the fulfillment of transport and communication requirements, the lightening of labor for men and women engaged in industry or in the home—these are objectives that every nation wants to attain. It is understandable that the peoples who today have almost nothing resent gloomy speculations about the undoubted blessings and the possible cost of the technical skill the race has acquired. Those who laid the foundations of scientific socialism have shown, however, that in the past, class inequality was essential in order that a minority might enjoy the comfort and leisure without which culture was impossible. Now an ever larger proportion of mankind is gaining access to culture—ultimately, all mankind. But our object in giving the masses of the future the luxury enjoyed in the past by the elite is to place culture within reach of all.

Only if this goal were achieved could scientific and technical rationality be confidently affirmed to be an advance in human progress in relation to the values of our day or those implicit in past civilizations. There is no certainty, however, that this will be so. The quality of existence is not determined by the amount of goods available to each person.

V

Apart from other considerations, many anthropologists and ethnologists have raised objections to the evolutionary philosophy that philosophers or sociologists often deduce from the undeniable fact of what we call scientific and technical development. The nature of these objections, the point at issue, and their scope may be seen in two booklets published by UNESCO, *Race and History,* by Claude Lévi-Strauss, and *Race and Culture,* by Michel Leiris,* both the authors being ethnologists of unquestioned repute. Much can be learned from these works, I think, for they are written concisely, with the general public in view, and reveal clearly the structure of the writers' thoughts, their historical judgments, and their value judgments.

The position adopted by ethnologists is interesting in that, in one important respect, it appears to be the same as that of the evolutionists. Comte said that the history of mankind should be thought of as the history of one nation. The two ethnologists mentioned stoutly deny the doctrine of racial inequality: "It is fruitless," writes Leiris, "to seek in the biology of race an explanation of the differences observable between the cultural achievements of the various peoples" (p. 37). A nation's capabilities do not remain constant. "The music, painting, and sculpture or architecture of some country will pass through a brilliant period and then for some centuries at least

* The page references that follow to both these works refer to their French editions, *Race et Histoire* (1952) and *Race et civilisation* (1951), and the quotations are translated directly from the French. [Ed.]

nothing further of any note will be produced" (p. 38). No culture is the product of a single race, nor is there any race whose cultural development has been uniform.

The conclusion Leiris draws from these propositions is that the scientific and technical superiority which Western culture enjoys at present is not due to racial factors or to the inheritance of races which have helped to build up Western civilization. And in support of this conclusion he indicates all that Western culture owes to other civilizations.

Lévi-Strauss speaks in the same strain. He shows that "cumulative" history is not the monopoly of Europe:

"Cumulative" history is not the prerogative of any one civilization or any one period. No doubt man first came to this great continent [the Americas] in small nomadic groups that crossed the Bering Straits during the final stages of the Ice Age, at some date which cannot have been much earlier than twenty thousand years ago. In twenty or twenty-five thousand years, these men produced one of the most amazing examples of "cumulative" history the world has ever seen: exploring the whole range of the resources of their new natural environment, cultivating a wide variety of plants (besides domesticating certain species of animals) for food, medicines, and poisons, and—as nowhere else—using poisonous substances as a staple article of diet (e.g., manioc) or as stimulants or anesthetics; collecting various poisons or drugs for use on the animal species that is particularly sensitive to each; and finally, developing certain industries, such as weaving, ceramics, and the working of precious metals, to the highest pitch of perfection. To appreciate this tremendous achievement, we need only assess the contribution America has made to the civilizations of the Old World, starting with the potato, rubber, tobacco, and coca (the basis of modern anesthetics), which are four fundamental, although admittedly very different, elements of Western culture, continuing with maize and ground-nuts, which were to revolutionize the economy of Africa before perhaps coming into general use in the diet in Europe, and cocoa, vanilla, the tomato, the pineapple, pepper, as well as several species of beans, cottons, and gourds. Finally, the zero, on the use of which arithmetic and, indirectly, modern mathematics are founded, was known and employed by the Maya at least 500 years before it was discovered by the Indian scholars from whom Europe received it via the Arabs (pp. 22-23).

Why is it that an evolutionary philosophy does not emerge from this essay on the equality of races? There appear to be two main reasons—the mechanism of change and the meaning given to the term "Western civilization."

Evolutionary philosophy presupposes a characteristic order of succession, a continuity of development, and a common aspiration to achieve a certain form of society. None of these features is to be found in the attitude toward history shown by these ethnologists. They believe that the achievements of civilization are the result of the combined efforts of a number of peoples and are stimulated if not actually engendered by contact and exchange among civilizations. "The peoples of Europe—whose overseas expansion, be it remembered, is of very recent date and is today restricted by the evolution of the very peoples they formerly surpassed in techniques—owed their cultural lead to the opportunities they have long had of frequent contacts among themselves and with contrasting groups" (Leiris, p. 39).

For his part, Lévi-Strauss disparages evolutionism (or *false* evolutionism) as "an attempt to wipe out the diversity of cultures while pretending to accord it full recognition. If the various conditions in which human societies are found, both in the past and in far distant lands, are treated as phases or stages in a single line of development, starting from the same point and leading to the same end, it seems clear that the diversity is merely apparent. Humanity is claimed to be one and the same everywhere" (p. 13). Lévi-Strauss puts forward a number of arguments of varying origin and scope against this false evolutionism. Evolutionist philosophy sees development as a regular, if not continuous, line; whereas Lévi-Strauss interprets human progress by referring to the biological theory of mutations: "Progress is neither continuous nor inevitable; its course consists of a series of leaps and bounds, or, as the biologists would say, mutations. These leaps and bounds are not always in the same direction; the general trend may change too, rather like the progress of the knight in chess, who always has several moves open to him but never in the same direction" (pp. 21-22). The great technical revolutions, those of the Neolithic age and of modern times—human or social mutations, so to speak, which emphasize the cumulative character of history —can be explained in terms of probabilities. The circumstances needed for such revolutions to take place hardly ever occur at the same time, just as a series of four or five consecutive numbers hardly ever turns up. And "a culture's chance of uniting the complex body of inventions of all sorts which we describe as a civilization depends on the number and diversity of the other cultures with which it is working out a common strategy, for the most part involuntarily" (p. 43).

In Lévi-Strauss's opinion, the evolutionist view is almost always artificial and reflects prejudice rather than valid interpretation. A few years ago, it was thought that the three techniques of the Paleolithic age—the "core tool," "flake tool," and "blade tool" industries—formed a sort of ladder like three stages of advance (lower, middle, and upper Paleolithic). "It is now recognized that these three variants were all found to-gether, representing not stages in a single advance, but aspects or facets of a technique which may not have been static but whose changes and variations were extremely complex" (p. 21). And again: "As our prehistoric and archaeological knowledge grows, we tend to make increasing use of a spatial scheme of distribution of civilizations that we once imagined in a temporal order" (p. 21).

Lastly, ethnologists condemn evolutionism because they do not regard Western civilization as a model for the whole world. It is obvious that Western civilization has enormously increased man's power over nature. It has outstripped other civilizations in the per-capita supply of energy and the protec-tion and prolongation of human life. But these are selected activities, particular centers of interest, and there are other ac-tivities, other centers of interest. "Progress never represents anything more than the maximum progress in a given direc-tion, predetermined by the interests of the observer" (p. 40).

Both Leiris and Lévi-Strauss, therefore, deny that it is pos-sible to establish a hierarchy of cultures. Each culture has its successes and failures, each is imperfect. But how can we assess the imperfections and the achievements except by adopting a system of values which would be the system obtaining in one particular civilization—that is, by taking as a standard one of the points on which we are trying to compare it with others? "The truth is that all cultures have their successes and failures, their faults and virtues" (Leiris, p. 41). Both writers cite nu-merous examples in support of their view that there can be no hierarchy of cultures. "The pre-Columbian Indian races, al-though they used no draft animals and had not invented the wheel or discovered iron, nevertheless left impressive monuments that testify to the existence of a highly developed social organization and that are among the finest works of man" (Leiris, p. 40). "If the criterion chosen were the degree of ability to overcome even the most inhospitable geographical conditions, there can be scarcely any doubt that the Eskimos, on the one hand, and the Bedouins, on the other, would win the prize. . . . As long as thirteen centuries ago, Islam formulated the theory that all aspects of human life—technological, economic, social, and spiritual—are closely interrelated—a theory that has only recently been rediscovered in the West in certain aspects of Marxist thought and in the development of modern ethnology" (Lévi-Strauss, p. 27). In matters touching on the organization of the family, the Australian aborigines are quite advanced; "the wealth and boldness of aesthetic imagination found in the Melanesians and their talent for embodying in social life the most obscure products of the mind's unconscious activity mark one of the highest peaks to which men have attained in these two directions" (p. 28).

Let us state the argument in abstract terms: if every society has its own type of "culture," its own *pattern,* societies are in essence not comparable, because the achievements of an industrial society have no place in the pattern of very many archaic or traditional societies. The "cultural model" disintegrates as soon as those who follow it adopt technical methods or beliefs which are incompatible with its particular logic. By superior strength, Western civilization has forced itself upon all other civilizations or societies with a different cultural pattern; the non-Western peoples yielded to this force—they were not converted by the light of truth.

There are a number of different elements in the ethnologists' anti-evolutionist philosophy. Broadly speaking, they are:

(1) the theory of the equality of the races of mankind; (2) the theory that historical change is the result of mutation, a rare and improbable conjunction of favorable circumstances, cooperation, communication, and conflict between groups of people; and (3) the theory that civilizations or types of culture are not comparable, since each sociocultural complex is defined by certain essential choices, which cannot be arranged in order of importance.

We shall not discuss the first theory, with which we are in general agreement. It is impossible to draw a direct parallel between cultural phenomena and biological or genetic data. Every civilization is the work of several races and several peoples. If, however, there is no proof of the basic inequality of the races of man, neither is there any proof of the equality of the races with regard to *all* the achievements of civilization. Within a population that is racially homogeneous, individuals are not all equally gifted, and it is conceivable that the various groups of mankind may not contain the same proportions of individuals capable of a particular type of activity or creative work.

The second and third elements in this philosophy are the most relevant to our theme—the relation between the modern theory of development and evolutionist philosophy. The first rules out an evolutionist theory of development for the future, and the second rules out the equation of the growth of knowledge and power with social and human progress, since Western society, which has progressed further than others *in one direction,* has at the same time failed to achieve other aspects of civilization or to attain other human virtues. No society can explore every path at once; each takes its place and expresses itself in one cultural model and is necessarily foreign to others.

In spite of appearances, the second of these two elements appears to me to be the most important. Ethnologists interpret the great revolutions of the Neolithic or industrial periods by the theory of mutations and chance. Professor Ginsberg claims that reason plays an active part in the historical phase and in the factors constituting a line of progress. Ethnologists would probably agree that, once the objective is decided upon, development takes place through reason. Rationalists might admit that cooperation between peoples and the coincidence of circumstances were, at least to some extent, essential factors in the outbreak of some of the great revolutions.

On the other hand, there seems to be a basic contradiction between the ethnologists' belief in the plurality of fundamentally different cultural patterns and the evolutionists' belief that progress will lead to rationalization which will gradually spread throughout the world. The contradiction seems to me to be undeniable, but it appears to be based on value judgments rather than on factual judgments.

Patterns of culture are many and varied. Each encourages the development of certain virtues and inhibits the manifestation of others. One civilization expresses itself through the mastery of the passions (India) and another through the mastery of the atom (the West). Does it follow that science's last word will be that there can be no hierarchy of cultures, no progress from Paleolithic man to modern man? I do not think so.

In one sense, there is no answer to the claim that a universally valid value judgment is not feasible, just as there is no answer to man's age-old skepticism. But the argument provides its own answer, it is its own undoing. The ethnologists we have quoted make numerous value judgments. Referring to wall paintings, Leiris says that their "beauty has never been exceeded"; he therefore believes that he is able to appreciate aesthetic values. Speaking of the Melanesians, Lévi-Strauss does not hesitate to declare that they reached "one of the highest peaks attained by men in this direction." Once the direction is decided upon, the height attained must be objectively measured. Why is it that these ethnologists think it impossible to set up a hierarchy of world civilizations or cultural patterns? Because they believe each of the patterns to be original and the result of a choice as to the work or activity considered essential. Seen from this angle, scientific knowledge or technical ability is only one task, one activity, among others. Furthermore, if the final criterion more or less consciously adopted by anthropologists is social integration, the societies of the past may appear to be in many ways superior to the societies of today, and archaic societies may even seem to be superior to historical societies. In short, if we are to return to the evolutionist viewpoint, we must stress the value of science and technology, that is, reason. If we do not, the pluralist viewpoint of the ethnologists is the only one possible.

If we accept the primacy of science and technology over other phases of human activity, are we clinging dogmatically to the values peculiar to the West and falling into the sin of inhumanity—contempt of our fellow men? I do not think so. To deny that science, technology, and reason have this primacy is to profess a philosophy which one does not really live out and to regard as meaningless the process by which man has slowly moved away from his original animal way of life to people the planet, master it, and possess it.

The anthropologist who formulates the thesis of the equality of cultural patterns bases his argument on truth as the immanent purpose of cogitation. He cannot deny that truth is superior to error. Now, the sciences of modern man are not one pattern among others, they are truer than those of other ages. Past civilizations never wished to entertain false ideas—they were not even indifferent to scientific truth. In this respect, Western civilization is superior to them when judged by the norms which ethnologists reject but which the men whom the ethnologists study would not have rejected, in principle if not in practice.

True knowledge and technical power are not merely aspects of culture or factors in a particular pattern; they have a universal vocation. Western culture conforms to a special pattern, but one which, by enabling scientific and technical reason to develop, *from a particular point of view* partakes of the virtual universality of reason. In the future, societies and civilizations that wish to survive will have to accept the social and mental *differentiation* which the development of reason demands. A mental and social universe in which science and religion, economy and politics, laws and customs are differentiated, and every activity has its own conceptual basis, is not, as a cultural pattern, superior to the universe of historic or prehistoric times. It may be less efficient at integrating the individual into the community and man's turbulent nature into a harmonious, peaceful life. If our aim is to ensure the happiness of the greatest number, perhaps it would have been better not to go any further than the stage of Bergson's closed societies. But in the last analysis, to prefer half-stationary societies to cumulative societies is to regard civilized man as no better than the first examples of Homo sapiens and to deny the value and significance of that process of change thanks to which the qualities generally acknowledged to be the essence of humanity have come into being and developed.

Evolutionist philosophy thought it had the answer to these questions. The theorists of development know—or ought to know—that they offer no answer but a restatement of old problems and also of problems that are peculiar to ourselves.

III

The End of Ideology and the Renaissance of Ideas

OPIUM OF THE INTELLECTUALS, which I wrote in 1954, the year following Stalin's death, appeared in 1955; the conclusion bore the title "The End of the Ideological Age?" (with a question mark). Since then, the themes of the end of ideology and industrial society have popularized to such an extent, and have given rise to so much comment and speculation, that I feel the desire not so much to define my ideas once again as to take stock of my position and re-examine my own views.

INDUSTRIAL SOCIETY AND ITS SYSTEMS

I

Marxist-Leninists dislike the concept of industrial society, for many easily understood reasons. The concept goes back to Saint-Simon, the Saint-Simonians, and Auguste Comte. Therefore, according to the idea of history that Pierre Vilar naïvely expounds, it has been rendered obsolete by the progress of Science. Saint-Simon, Comte, and Tocqueville belong to a now outdated past, whereas Marx is our contemporary and his thought is still considered representative of the present state of science. Since Socialism is supposed to mark the end of prehistory, Marxist-Leninists will not admit that it is only one among various forms of government or that it can figure, with capitalism, among the varieties of modern society. Finally, the comparison of socialism and capitalism raises difficulties for them, since Soviet socialism, the system of the future, is obviously eager to "catch up" with American capitalism, which is doomed. How can such a discrepancy be explained within a theory based on the primacy of the productive forces?

This explains why most Marxist speakers spend their time attacking a thesis which no one has ever defended—that there is one form of industrial society and only one, an absurd doctrine that is tantamount to denying the important differences between systems. In an interview (published by *Arts*), Henri Lefebvre allowed himself a further flight of imagination, maintaining that I "launched the somewhat confused idea of a single or world-wide industrial society" and that I am now criticizing that idea myself. In point of fact, what I criticize is not the "somewhat confused idea" but the confused interpretation put upon a simple, commonplace idea by many people. As for self-criticism, I am willing to leave it to Lefebvre, since he is so good at it.

Vilar, on the other hand, confines himself to a so-called historical analysis of the success of what he terms the theory of industrial society. He claims that this theory has been gaining ground since 1954, that is, since the Soviet Union exploded its first hydrogen bomb (one wonders why the explosion of the first atomic bomb was not enough to start the process), and cites Herbert Marcuse and Pierre Naville, both of whom are Marxist by training and still, to some extent, Marxist in allegiance (but not Marxist-Leninist). The achievements of the Soviet Union, he says, have induced bourgeois sociologists to camouflage capitalism by calling it industrial society and to admit the Soviet Union to the ranks of the developed countries.

This argument, although crude, does contain an element of truth. In the long run, the facts have to be accepted, even by fanatics. It is obvious that systems that claim to be irrevocably hostile to each other have built up industries whose production techniques (in Marxist terms, the productive forces) are similar. It was inevitable, therefore, that economists, sociologists, and philosophers should begin to study general political economy as if capitalist and socialist economies were only particular instances of it, and to study industrial society or civilization as a whole. According to Vilar, "the substitution of the praise of science and technology for the praise of capitalism" is symptomatic of a "profound change of attitude, . . . [but] not the kind of limited change which would encourage the analysts of industrial society, remembering previous errors, to be prudent." It would be easy to retort that this piece of advice, coming as it does from an ex-Stalinist, is itself imprudent, not to say impudent. Sputniks can hardly be said to cancel out the personality cult.

But enough of cheap polemics. Has there been a "profound change of attitude," as Vilar claims? Where did science and modern technology originate and flourish, if not in Western Europe, first under the monarchies, then under bourgeois regimes? Depending on the circumstance or the reigning school of thought, capitalist or Western ideology has extolled the virtues of private property and individual initiative, or the creative power of science and technology. Marx himself praised the great achievements of the conquering bourgeoisie, which, in the space of a single century, did more to transform the world than any other class of exploiters had done in thousands of years. I admit that Western nations prefer the adjective "industrial" to "capitalist," just as the Soviets refer to themselves as "socialists" whereas we refer to them as "totalitarians." Until we banish from scientific terminology all terms taken from modern jargon, each of us is at liberty to "unmask" the political or ideological aims concealed behind a given vocabulary.

The fact remains that Western societies, in so far as they developed according to capitalist doctrines or have tried to become truly capitalist, have also been actuated by the spirit of science or technology. This is not to deny that some Western thinkers have felt a nostalgic longing for the old order and have expressed a horror of technology, which robs nature of its charms and the countryside of its poetry; but, while such schools of thought may occasionally have slowed down the process of change, they have never checked it altogether. The voices from the past found support only during periods of crisis, when the means of production seemed to exceed the absorptive capacity of the market, and when science caused widespread unemployment and poverty.

The truth is that neither the explosion of the H-bomb nor even Stalin's death was instrumental in popularizing the concept of industrial society; at least equally responsible for this was the success achieved by the Western economies, European ones in particular. Countries west of the Iron Curtain have been free from economic depression since 1945: even the United States, whose growth was on several occasions interrupted by periods of recession, has not experienced any economic crisis in the nineteenth-century, or more especially in the 1929, sense.

Since the war, two facts—the Soviet Union's build-up of manufacturing industries under state control and independent of private ownership of the instruments of production, and the continuous and rapid development achieved by Western countries (since 1950 the rate of growth in the West has been higher than it was during the preceding century or even at the beginning of this century)—have, as it were, made comparison unavoidable.

This comparison may often betray ulterior political motives, but in itself it is a neutral process. Doctrinaire thinkers on both sides are irritated to find themselves in undesirable company, but they are wrong; the fact that both societies can be classed as industrial does not mean that the Western and the Soviet (or, if you like, capitalist and socialist) systems are in any sense identical. Only a technological interpretation of history would allow us to assert that all societies that use atomic energy and computers are the same. It is absurd to state as a foregone conclusion that what they have in common is more important than the differences between them.

To begin with, one should endorse the sensible remarks of Alfred Sauvy: "Certain points . . . seem to me to be undeniable: there exist two systems; they have certain features in common and they show marked differences. The common features are numerous and obvious, especially as regards technical and even social problems. On the other hand, the differences are easy to see, and some of them are fundamental."

The concept of *industrial society* raises three fundamental problems: 1) How are we to define industrial society? Is the term appropriate? Is there not already such a thing as post-industrial society? (2) Where exactly, at the present moment, do the essential differences between the two types of system occur, and how significant are these differences? (3) Are the two types of system becoming more and more alike as they develop? Is it true, as Maurice Duverger tells us, that the society of the future will be a democratic socialist system toward which Western societies will move through a process of socialization and Soviet societies through a process of liberalization?

By industrial society, *I do not mean a historically unique society, or a specific period in contemporary societies, but a type of society which appears to open up a new era in human experience.* The concept of industrial society is comparable to that of archaic society, presenting the same advantages and the same difficulties. It is easy to give a rough definition of the features of a certain type of society, and difficult to define its exact limits and to assert that it is, or is not, archaic or industrial. A complex society which is also illiterate is, or is not, archaic, according to the definition adopted. The very nature of an industrial society only adds to the difficulties. We are able to observe archaic societies, even those which exist at present and which now continue to live and evolve as if they belonged to the past, but industrial society is still in a primitive stage.

Furthermore, societies of the industrial type think of themselves as evolving in time; they are what they will be. Soviet society maintains that it cannot be understood if observers consider only its present state and fail to recognize that the socialism of the future alone gives meaning to the present.

It would perhaps have been preferable to substitute the expression "industrial type of society" or possibly "industrial culture" or "civilization" for the term "industrial society." I began by using the term "civilization," which had the advantage of suggesting those achievements which all modern societies have in common and of avoiding Aristotelian logic (according to which industrial society would be the genus of which Soviet and Western societies were species), which I do not find entirely satisfactory. But the objection was raised that, while we correctly refer to Chinese, Indian, or American cultures as civilizations, in the expression "industrial civilization" the latter word is used in the singular but the qualifying adjective does not refer to an historical entity.

Such linguistic quibbles have little interest for me and would be of no concern if they did not give rise to intellectual confusion and verbal controversies. The question at issue is how to determine the essential constituent elements of this type of society. Now, on this point the Saint-Simonians seem to me to have taken the right view; at any rate, Saint-Simonian ideas, in the form given to them by Auguste Comte, are still relevant. All human societies have enjoyed a certain degree of technical knowledge and skill. But so great is the quantitative inequality between the scientific knowledge of ancient or medieval societies and that of American or Soviet society today, and between their degrees of technical skill, that it is tantamount to a difference in kind. In this sense, the type of society which, following many other writers, I have called industrial, could also be called scientific. Science and technology have made it possible for 3 billion human beings to live on this earth, for the standard of living to rise from year to year in advanced countries, and for famine to be avoided, even in the underdeveloped countries where the population sometimes increases by 2 or 3 per cent a year. The *qualitative* difference between present-day and earlier science and technology is *obviously* the indispensable precondition of all the other features usually attributed to modern societies: the lengthening of the life-span, the steady increase in national output, the predominant and at times obsessional concern with production and expansion, the creation of an artificial environment for human life, vast labor and administrative organizations, specialization, intellectual and social rationalization, etc. It would be easy to show that none of the phenomena that observers consider essential to modern society would be possible without the development of science and technology.

But the existence of this prerequisite does not always point to the essential issue, or, rather, there are various ways of considering what is essential. Comte simplified the problem by postulating that a society normally has one objective (at least one main objective) and one only, and that it also has only one way of thinking. According to Comte's postulate, the exploitation of natural resources replaces wars of conquest, just as peaceful pursuits replace war, and science, metaphysics and theology (although ultimately a form of religion is seen as emerging from science). After the experience of the last century, no one can continue to accept this postulate, although Comte is still right on two points: thanks to the application of science, the productive capacity of labor reduces or abolishes the economic rationality of conquest and colonies; and the destructive power of military weapons adds to the irrationality of wars, which become more costly and less profitable for the conquerors themselves.

It does not follow, however, that the industrial type of society is adequately defined solely by its scientific spirit. For the peoples who have felt the impact of Western civilization and who dread, admire, or detest the achievements of the West, science is first and foremost the source of technology. It expresses the will to power rather than the quest for truth and wisdom. Yet, for the scientists themselves, for those who genuinely belong to the scientific community, science depends on cooperation between theory and experience, and this cooperation demands equally the disinterestedness of pure speculation and modesty—i.e., the kind of humility that asks questions and abides by nature's reply.

This theoretical scientific spirit has no connection with a shopkeeper's careful sums, or the Puritan's thrift and savings (time is money), or the banker's buying and selling of shares, or the physicist's development of the atomic bomb and ballistic missiles, or the attitude of the men of the Apollo project, whose dream is to send astronauts to the moon. When Spengler called the Western mind "Faustian," he illuminated at least one feature of the culture in which industrial society has developed. Similarly, when Toynbee presents science and technology as separate fragments of the historical entity that he calls the Christian civilization of the West, he is suggesting, and perhaps rightly so, that there may be tenuous or indirect links between a system of transcendental beliefs and the knowledge that is typical of our day and age.

Viewed from the outside, objectively, all societies of the industrial type have technology—that is to say, to a certain extent at least, science—as their fundamental precondition. But "collective economic man," who thanks to technology has been able to exploit the riches of nature, has never been characterized by the disinterestedness of the scientist exclusively concerned with truth; even for the scientist or scholar, the concern with truth can take various forms and be prompted by various passions. Historians and sociologists have described many types of entrepreneurs, and the discussion of the affinities between Puritanism and capitalism has recently been revived on the occasion of the Weber centenary. It involves two closely linked yet distinguishable problems: one is the problem of historical causality (to what extent did certain Puritans participate in the creation of capitalism?); the other is the problem of spiritual affinity (are the Puritan and capitalist mentalities closely related, are they activated by a similar spirit?).

Even today, it would be useless to try to discover some spirit common to the Chairman and Managing Director of a big American corporation, a wealthy French farmer, an English industrialist educated at Eton and Oxford, and the Communist Party member who is director of a Soviet trust. But to the degree that industrialization leads to greater rationalization, business enterprises develop more and more common features. They must calculate expenses, receipts, profits, and taxes; the calculations must cover a certain duration—since the production cycle itself requires time; all the elements of the balance-sheet must be translated into comparable quantities—and thus, no essential distinction can be established between the cost of manpower and that of material. Man is replaced by the machine when figures prove that this would be profitable. In this respect, not only capitalist society but any society treats man as if he were a commodity or as an instrument of production.

A quantitative and uniform formulation of labor costs

(wages) and cost in materials and time (rates of interest, anticipated yield from investments over a given period) is imperative in all modern economies. Without corresponding to the essence of the scientific spirit, this organization of collective labor uses instruments provided by science and conforms to a method inspired by science.

But quantification and prognosis remain a form of rationalization of *means.* Are the *aims* of industrial societies clearly defined? Here we come back to Comte's postulate: agreed that henceforth all societies of the industrial type are eager to exploit the resources of their natural environment, what is their aim in doing so? We know that, at least in the present transitional period, there are two possibilities: the material well-being of the few or the many; and the power and prestige of the community as a whole. In a way, the plurality of aims that societies may pursue echoes and simplifies the plurality of attitudes characteristic of entrepreneurs at various periods and in various nations. Just as an entrepreneur strives to achieve his chosen ends—profit, the prosperity of his family business, success as proof of his ability, or the joy of creation—so each society puts its system of production at the service of some ideal, although it may not always be aware of its nature.

At the present time, and in the abstract, the two hostile camps both maintain their aim to be the happiness and prosperity of the greatest number. The Soviet leaders have never admitted any ambition other than the building of a socialist state, and this has always implied abundance and well-being. But, in fact, until quite recently, concern for the general well-being of the citizens seemed to be subordinated to the desire to increase output at all costs or to strengthen the collective power. Let us leave aside for the time being the question of whether this priority was accidental or necessary. We will merely note that, when defined in terms of its productive or destructive capacity, industrial society does not in and of itself have an ultimate aim. It is powerful as regards achieving the objective assigned by its leaders. Generally speaking, this productive capacity has been stimulated both by regimes that depend on individual initiative to ensure that each citizen is rewarded according to his abilities, within a general context of prosperity, and by other systems that rely on planning and state control and reject on principle the private ownership of the instruments of production. The American dream, heir to the Enlightenment philosophy of eighteenth-century Europe, is far removed from Soviet ideology, a voluntarist interpretation of Marxist Prometheanism. But the individual American is not solely inspired by the American dream, any more than the individual Soviet citizen by the ideal of a socialist state. At all levels of society, under capitalism and socialism alike, there is a mixture of motives in the consciousness of each individual. It would be childish to suggest that American citizens are more self-seeking than Soviet citizens simply because the United States' system of government relies on competition and the Soviet Union's on state planning.

If modern societies have science and technology as their basic precondition, although not as their spiritual essence, and if, at first sight at least, they appear to have no common aim, why do we speak of the industrial type of society and in what sense do we include in it societies whose economic and social systems, like their cultural standards, are different? I repeat that, following Comte, I am taking the word "industry" in a broad, not narrow, sense—to include any kind of collective effort transformed by the application of scientific method or the scientific spirit. This use of the word is not contrary to modern usage, since we talk about the industrialization of agriculture—the simplest manifestations of which are strict accountancy, large-scale investment, mechanization, and seed selection, and the most complex is, or will be, factory-produced food, involving the smallest possible use of ground-space. (In this sense, the rearing of chickens is already industrialized, and the principle is being applied to other forms of livestock.) If we take the word "industry" in this sense, the concept of a post-industrial society appears to me to be superfluous and even unfortunate. It is open to objection from the Marxists, who accuse us of defining types of society by technology alone, or by historically unspecified terms (such as "industry"). Computers no doubt open up a new era in technology, just as the steam-engine and electricity did in the past, but technological eras and phases are not enough to define a type of society. Already, the industrial society involves administration as much as production, and the effects of automation on administration as well as production will undoubtedly change our working methods and modes of life. But it does not necessarily follow that we are emerging from an industrial type of society into a new one.

Even if we conceive of industry in the narrow sense, the concept of a post-industrial society would still seem open to criticism. Industry remains the foundation of modern societies, even if increased productivity makes it possible to reduce the percentage of labor used in the primary and secondary sectors. Indeed, such a reduction seems to me to correspond to the nature of industrial society and consequently represents a normal development and not a break with the past or a change of direction. The more scientifically organized production is, the greater the part played by machines and then by administration. The so-called "post-industrial" period, precisely because the high productivity of labor in factories producing its primary and secondary goods will remain one of its indispensable pre-conditions, will emphatically belong to the type I call industrial. And a basically tertiary-sector society, devoted to services, will also have as its basis the production of material goods.

This terminology, it seems to me, avoids some of the difficulties that have been raised in various quarters. Where does so-called industrial society begin and end? From what point are we entitled to call a society industrial? None of these questions admits of a categorical answer. Many phenomena that appear inseparable from the industrial type of society did not occur until the twentieth century. In every age, industrialization is organized according to the means that science places at the disposal of the producers. Certain sociologists have singled out technological periods; others, economic and social systems. Such "periodization" or "classification" is in theory legitimate, but can be contested. Debate now centers on the historical or human significance of the various typologies. Today, the most popular subject for discussion is obviously the resemblances and differences—or the possible convergence—between the Soviet and Western systems.

II

The convergence theory is becoming increasingly widespread in the West (but not in the Soviet Union, at least not officially). Maurice Duverger, who is sensitive to intellectual fashions, confirms this in his latest book, *Introduction à la pol-*

itique. "In fact, a transformation in depth is slowly bringing them closer together. The Soviet Union and the peoples' democracies will never turn capitalist, the United States and Western Europe will never turn Communist, but both sides seem to be moving toward socialism through a two-fold progression of liberalization in the East and socialization in the West." Thus we can expect the mutually hostile systems to come together at some unspecified date in a form of "democratic socialism." *

In order that this theory should not be accused of being conservative or reactionary, Duverger rounds it off with three assertions, which he calls three substantial facts: "the technical superiority of planned productivity over capitalist production; the impossibility of building up a real human community on the basis of capitalist principles; finally, the devalorization of these principles." † The first assertion represents a point of view that most economists would consider false or even absurd. The second contains a certain element of truth but poses a problem without putting forward any kind of solution: the pursuit of self-interest is not peculiar to capitalism; the competitive spirit is no less keen under a Communist regime than under a capitalist one, but simply takes different forms, and it is no easy matter to determine which forms are preferable, or least obnoxious. The third assertion also contains an element of truth, although it leaves undefined the precise respects in which the principles of capitalism have lost their validity.

Curiously enough, Duverger finds capitalism inferior in those departments in which its superiority is usually admitted.

* *Introduction à la politique* (Paris, 1964), p. 367.
† Ibid., p. 371.

For instance, according to him, "American economists themselves are aware of the inferiority of capitalism in the tertiary sector." * If we remember that commerce forms part of the tertiary sector, and if we have some knowledge, however slight, of the commercial agencies of East European countries, we cannot but marvel at this assertion. It is true that many public services can be satisfactorily maintained only through collective ownership and the abandonment of the profit principle—in other words by "socialist" methods. No believer in modern liberalism has ever questioned the fact that the state should ensure certain social services. But the question is *which* services? The American telephone system, by far the best in the world, is operated strictly along profit-making lines.

The other argument used to justify the superiority of socialism is not much better. "Total planning," it is said, would be impossible in the capitalist framework; also, "the losses resulting from a planned economy are less serious than those which occur through the enormous wastage in advanced capitalist economies." Planning "substitutes normal, coherent, oriented progress for the aberrant movements of capitalist economy, which are like the twitches of vivisected animals." † Not one of these propositions is not equivocal, dubious, or wrong. Planning undoubtedly makes it possible to determine objectives, grant priorities to certain undertakings (as capitalist states can do too), and increase the percentage of investment in the national output (not so easily done by capitalism, but in any case why need it, in principle, sacrifice the present generation for the sake of the future?). But there is no guarantee that the objectives determined, or the decisions made, by political lead-

* *Loc. cit.*
† Ibid., p. 375.

ers (who exercise supreme authority over the planners) will be judicious. Compared to the losses caused by the Soviet leaders' mistakes (e.g., the attempt to cultivate the virgin lands of Central Asia), the wastage under capitalism seems in fact slight.

Enough of such "substantial facts" and sweeping statements. How does the problem of "convergence" really present itself?

The problem can only be stated by the use, and abuse, of what are called "schematic simplifications" or "ideal-types." The first simplification consists in concentrating on three specific fields—economy, politics, and ideology—and especially on the system of values associated with the first two. A second simplification consists in deciding on some option in each field which we consider as being either inherently decisive or decisive in relation to what our particular interests are. In the economic field, the complex of institutions and activities whereby the community, in its struggle against nature, creates and shares scarce resources, three options are held to be decisive: the ownership of the means of production, regulatory methods (the allocation of resources and the ensuring of a supply-demand equilibrium), and the distribution of income among individuals and groups.

1. As far as the ownership of the instruments of production is concerned, nothing justifies an assertion that the Western and Soviet systems will come to resemble each other. Unless we agree that the huge American corporations are collectively owned—and this would not be incompatible with a certain kind of Marxism—we have no grounds (political accidents apart) for anticipating that state ownership will become general in Western industry, still less so in agriculture and commerce, the two sectors in which Soviet methods have most

obviously failed. Certain social services are and will remain state-owned, and here and there, subject to the ups and downs of political party warfare, some sectors will come under partial or total state control. Social legislation (of which Social Security is the prototype) will continue and will probably become more widespread, although the state may be forced on financial grounds to limit the expenditure and the categories of beneficiaries and leave more to be done by cooperative or mutual-aid societies.

2. As regards regulatory methods, the most likely possibility appears to be a gradual abandonment in the East of the Soviet-type centralized and authoritarian planning, and a return to the mechanism of the market, which is necessary for adjusting prices in accordance with demand and not simply with production costs. (This forecast is by no means certain: in making it, I am influenced by the debates now going on in the Soviet Union and in Eastern Europe, as well as by what I hold to be desirable and effective. Economic revisionism is very much in evidence at the moment in Soviet reviews and journals, but it has not been adopted by the Party and has even been officially rejected.)

Does this revisionism imply a break with the Marxism of Marx? Did total planning originate in a particular interpretation of *Das Kapital*? Interesting though this question is, it is really too complex and technical to be dealt with *en passant*. Peter Wiles is undoubtedly right when he maintains* that Soviet practices in many cases derive directly from Marx's writings or from the logical implications of these texts. In criticizing capitalism, Marx indicated what socialism ought *not* to be,

* *The Political Economy of Communism* (Oxford: Basil Blackwell, 1952).

but statements relating to socialism are too scattered and vague to add up to a theory. As long as the instruments of production are publicly owned and the state retains control of production and distribution, the planners—even if they recognize the effects of scarcity and what is involved in a rational allocation of resources, and even if they use the profit principle as a guide —can still claim to be faithful to the Founder, although they may not be following the literal text of *Das Kapital*.

3. Finally, as regards the distribution of income, two main problems emerge: the degree of inequality, and the degree of freedom that individuals are allowed in the use of their wealth. In theory, if all workers were employed by the state—in other words, if all the instruments of production were collectively owned and the planners were in complete control of the economy—inequality of income would be reduced by the political authorities to a level they decided on or judged necessary (the purpose of inequality being to serve as an incentive, for the young while they were still learning and for adults at work). In fact, in present-day Soviet society, the scale of incomes does not correspond to this ideal pattern. The range of wages and salaries widened during the period of Stalin's five-year plans and has since become somewhat narrower, but the difference in standards, more especially in the standard of living, remains considerable between the managerial classes and the workers. When measured in terms of rubles or dollars, the gap is less than that which exists in the United States between a road-sweeper and the managing director of a great corporation or the heir to a large family fortune, yet it may be *qualitatively* greater, since in the United States many goods (including housing) are within reach of the average income, whereas the general shortage of resources in the Soviet Union means that

certain commodities which in an advanced Western country would be widely distributed are reserved for a minority. Furthermore, in Soviet society there are other kinds of inequality that the planners tolerate, although they neither intended nor approve of them: e.g., variations of income from one *kolkhoz* to another according to the fertility of the land, or from one factory to another according to the degree of efficiency of the organization or organizer.

Another problem, as important as the problem of inequality, concerns the method of distribution of income. Granted a certain total national output, it is divided, in the first place, between investment and consumption (a division that is determined by the planners, since the tax on the annual turn-over provides most of the national savings); secondly, between the capital allocated to heavy industry and that allocated to light industry; thirdly, between the amount available for consumption which individuals are free to allocate as they choose and the amount the state allocates to consumption through various administrative channels.* This last division of consumer goods is not unknown in the West: the cost of social security within the total cost of labor illustrates the significance of the concept of "the distribution, through administrative channels, of that part of the national income which the community assigns to consumption." In the program drawn up by the Twenty-Second Congress of the Communist Party of the U.S.S.R., collective consumption was estimated at half of the total.

If we consider these three variables—the form of ownership, the method of regulating the economy and allocating resources, and the distribution of wealth—we are at once aware

---

* This tripartite analysis is of course a logical one and does not represent an actual order.

of considerable, indeed fundamental, differences between the
two systems, as ideal-types. In the East, collective ownership is
general; there is centralized, authoritarian planning, without
market prices, which aims at ensuring the highest possible rate
of growth, with priority for heavy industry; private incomes
are limited and a considerable proportion of them distributed
by the state since inequality is reduced, in principle though not
in fact, to the minimum necessary for the efficient working of
the economy. In the West, various forms of ownership are
maintained; the obvious aim of the economy is to raise the
standard of living, and prices are recognized as being a necessary mechanism and, indeed, as a measure of rationality, although governments, in various ways, keep a check on, and
occasionally rectify, the functioning of the market economy.
Opinions differ about how much should be allocated for individual consumption and how much for public expenditure, but
many observers believe that the latter should diminish as individuals come to earn incomes high enough to enable them to
choose their own way of life and insure themselves against
accidents. (I am not sure that this is a majority view, and the
discussion about "social services" vs. gadgetry, "artificially
stimulated needs," or the buying of useless products is marked
by ambiguity and passion.)

The convergence theory, then, if we limit ourselves to eco-
nomics alone, presupposes either an increasing similarity between the forms of ownership, the methods of regulating the
economy, and the distribution of income, or a dwindling importance for the differences that cannot be eliminated. I have
suggested a possible increasing similarity of the second—
methods of control—since Soviet planners gradually have had
to strengthen the autonomy of individual plants and result to

the profit index (which entails re-creating a market economy, abandoning the artificial fixing of prices of goods, and, finally, acknowledging the role of scarcity and the concept of marginal efficiency of capital as indispensable for a rational allocation of resources). Should this hypothesis prove correct, the two systems will tend to converge in this particular sphere, not, as Duverger says, because Western countries will come to acknowledge the superiority of a total planned economy, but, on the contrary, because the Soviet Union will eventually admit that the conceptual apparatus used by Marx and Ricardo is an anachronism and that the marginalist argument not only is valid in the case of capitalism but is essential for any modern economy. Western economies no longer belong to the free market, but to a "controlled-market" type. The state intervenes in order to maintain an over-all balance and to prevent inflation and periods of depression, so as, in the long run, to increase the amount of investment, to give preference to particular investments or certain sectors that are held to be of national importance, to rectify the unequal distribution of income that results from the market economy, and to finance whatever social services or amenities are considered essential or desirable.

In the event of the Soviet regime moving away from centralized, authoritarian planning toward a less rigid system of planning with a market mechanism (or approximating to the Western "controlled-market" pattern), would the convergence of the two systems in their entirety necessarily follow? The machine equipment is the same or in the long run will differ very little more than it does already from one capitalist country to another; the organization of business is technically comparable; the goods produced will tend to be the same, although the Soviet regimes reject or are slow to adopt certain characteristically Western developments such as motorization. Everything points to the fact that durable consumer goods— refrigerators and washing machines, etc., i.e., inventions that ease the housewife's burden—will be as much in demand in Communist nations as in capitalist countries; already radios and television sets are no less in evidence in the East than in the West. At a similar point in their development, two countries, one with a Soviet, the other with a Western system, would be more alike than the two Europes are today.

But there is still the foreseeable clash between the different forms of ownership and methods of income distribution. Forms of ownership cannot be reduced to the simple alternative of public or private; Mr. Wiles lists ten types. In Western countries, we can note at least half a dozen different patterns: individual ownership, with an owner-manager; ownership by shareholders of limited companies, the manager or director not always being a major shareholder; state ownership of large firms (for instance Renault) or public service; ownership by consumers' cooperatives or producers' cooperatives; ownership by municipalities which are custodians and managers of the public services. In the Soviet Union, two types monopolize the entire economy: collective ownership, under strict state administration, the independence of various plants being reduced to a minimum; and the so-called cooperative ownership of the *kolkhoz;* a *kolkhoz,* however, is run on authoritarian lines, and the individual ownership of only very small allotments gives little justification for the use of the word "cooperative" in this case.

In the present controversy—and once again Duverger is admirably representative of the spirit of the times—the argu-

ment revolves around the alternative of public or private ownership, and the Soviet system is taken as representative of the
former. If the possible restoration of the market mechanism
becomes a reality in Eastern Europe—and it cannot unless industrial and business units are financially independent—public
ownership of the Soviet type will approximate to public ownership in the West, either of a single company or of a complex
of companies (e.g., Electricité de France). At that point, the
problem will consist of determining the advantages and disadvantages of (1) limited companies or public enterprises (or to
use Mr. Wiles' terms, managerial capitalism or managerial socialism); and (2) variety or uniformity in types of ownership.

Individual ownership is not incompatible with efficiency either in industry, commerce, or agriculture, although small
concerns in this category sometimes slow down the growth rate
and complicate the planners' task. However, the disadvantages
which ensue when the category is ruthlessly eliminated seem
greater than those which occur when it is allowed to survive
and adjust to new conditions. The nationalization of commerce, as experience has shown, is prejudicial to the interests
and convenience of consumers; agrarian collectivization has
met with more failure than success—even where it did not
bring about catastrophe, such as occurred in the Soviet Union
—and, while the industrialization of agriculture calls for rationalization and large-scale farming, it does not call for the
abolition of private ownership; but, lastly, in industry, particularly in heavy industry, the alternative of private ownership
or managerial capitalism on the one hand, and managerial or
state socialism on the other still holds good. Yet here, too,
reason urges that we should take certain issues into considera-

tion: the selection of managers according to the form of ownership; the manner in which, and the degree of efficiency with which, industrial enterprises are run as a result of this selection and the form of ownership; and, lastly, the question of human relations, the attitude of the workers to management as it may vary according to the legal definition of the form of ownership.*

Let us begin by dismissing a number of demagogic sophisms as they are expressed, again, by Duverger:

> In Europe, ownership of industries and businesses appears more and more in its true light—as power over men, hereditary power. For his employees, the capitalist is a leader, a ruler. Workers and employees are subject to his authority much more than they are to the state's. . . . Admittedly, every business and every organization, whether capitalist or not, needs to have someone in charge; but the fundamental nature of capitalist industry and business is that in it authority rests on the same divine right as that which was the foundation of power in the state centuries ago. †

It is true that there are still some businesses run by men who inherited their position. This is true of Ford in the United States and of Michelin and Peugeot in France. But, in the West, large corporations that keep to the pattern of family inheritance are more and more the exception to the rule, and even though there may be *many* such exceptions, they are possible only in those instances where the heirs show the necessary ability.

---

* There is a fourth issue—the incomes of managers or owners—which will be dealt with in the next section, where I shall discuss the distribution of wealth.

† Duverger, *op. cit.*, pp. 377–78.

But more important, one should examine whether, and to what extent, the character of those in control, the nature of their authority, and the attitude of the employees vary according to the system of ownership. As a matter of fact, the authority invested in Soviet managers or in the directors of state-owned concerns in the West is not basically different from that enjoyed by owner-managers of private businesses. Sociologists observed no change in the attitude of the workers in the Renault factories when Renault was nationalized. Soviet factories, where trade-union officials are not elected but appointed from above, show no signs of democratization or liberalization of worker-management relations.

In other words, all modern firms are organized on an authoritarian basis. Nowhere are the managing directors elected, or chosen, by those over whom they are set in control, and the kind of industrial reform desired by Bloch-Lainé in France, for instance—which Duverger calls the Orleanist solution—has as yet no equivalent on the other side of the Iron Curtain. In the East, there are no hereditary owners, but the power invested in the representatives of the state and the party is, in the way it is applied, nearer to divine right than is the power wielded by heads of firms in Western countries, who are subject to pressure from unions, public opinion, the press, the state, and even the church, which is careful to dissociate itself from big financial interests. Although collectivization of the Soviet type does away with the inheritance of managerial power, it nevertheless intensifies, rather than diminishes, its authoritarian nature.

Can we say that the attitude of employees—that is, of the workers—toward employers or managers alters with the disappearance of a hereditary body of employers and their replacement by the socialist conception of the single-party state? I hesitate to give a definite answer. It may be that, as conditions improve, workers in Russia will tend to identify their country with the regime, since the latter will gain credit for building up the socialist state. But so far, it does not appear that the political system of Eastern Europe is accepted by the mass of the population, and, in the Soviet Union itself, it is not yet able to withstand the free discussion of ideas that Western regimes, although they supposedly exploit and oppress the people, can tolerate without much risk.

Perhaps the two systems show a common tendency to make appointments according to ability (a Saint-Simonian conception) in industrial as well as state administration, but the method of selection is not necessarily the same, and the consequences of the method adopted—managerial capitalism or managerial socialism—may be significant. As regards the techno-bureaucratic direction of industries, it is at present authoritarian rather than democratic under all types of systems. The theory of spontaneous democratization has never been proved, although, in one way or another, all systems aim at encouraging the integration of the workers, or at least at giving them the feeling that they are fairly treated.*

On the issues of allocating national resources, distributing wealth, and eliminating inequality, can it be said that the two

---

* I am well aware that the terms *authoritarianism, democratization,* and *integration* are ambiguous. By authoritarianism I mean a situation in which the mass of the workers are undeniably organized and hierarchically controlled so that they cannot question and do not always understand. The workers' representatives discuss social problems and are kept informed of the firm's economic problems. Decisions, at least the major ones, continue to be taken by the managing director in conjunction with his staff. I doubt whether things could be organized differently and I am not even sure that they ought to be. Besides, in France, authority is challenged by the managerial classes and the intellectuals rather than by the workers and their representatives. By integration I mean merely the feeling of belonging to the business and accepting its aims.

systems are likely to converge and form a hybrid drawn equally from both? Let us suppose—although the possibility is still only hypothetical—that the desire to maximize the growth rate and to give priority to heavy industry gradually yields to the desire to grant to the present generation what, until now, had been promised only to future generations. Khrushchev proclaimed that "butter in the spinach," or "sturdy leather shoes," or "Hungarian goulash" provides an agreeable complement to collective ownership and the pre-eminence of the party. The day will come when it will cease to be a dogma that 25 per cent of the national income must be reinvested. Similarly, instead of continuing to echo the formula by which Marx defined capitalism—"Accumulate, accumulate, that is the Law and the Prophets"—the Soviet leaders will decide, when the time is ripe, that socialist integration (which mitigated the effects of the absence of capitalism, at least in Russia) has progressed far enough to allow the standard of living to be raised and an increase in consumption to be given priority. Such a change of policy is not as easily accomplished as is sometimes imagined in Western countries, since it involves at least an implicit recognition of the consumer's sovereignty.

Two queries remain: Will the party agree to foster individualism in consumption—that is, to allow each individual to spend his income as he pleases? Or will it on the contrary try to increase the amount of income subject to collective, authoritarian distribution, as the program of the Twelfth Congress suggested? The raising of living and cultural standards strengthens the desire for a personal and family life, and privileged members of Soviet society want motor-cars just as much as the bourgeoisie or workers in Western countries do. The pauperization thesis is just as erroneous when applied to the Soviet system as when applied to capitalist countries, but its application in Communist nations suffers from a contradiction unknown in the West: the monopoly enjoyed by the party, its privileges, and even some of its functions become less and less justifiable as the economy expands in accordance with what is called the building of socialism.

Of course, just as the hereditary owner bases his legitimacy on the argument that someone must be in charge (which is undeniable) and that the problem is which method of selecting leaders to choose, the *apparatchik* will say that all advanced societies require a political staff to run them (which is equally undeniable) and that recruitment through the party is the best method. Nevertheless, there is a difference. Hereditary heads of firms do not enjoy a monopoly and, in the event of maladministration, are subject to the reactions of the market. Members of the Communist Party hierarchy have a monopoly on political activity and enjoy a position superior to that of technicians and managers, although Soviet society claims and declares that it is actuated by the scientific spirit.

"The citizens of the Soviet state," we are told,

> want to enjoy life, to make the most of the present, and to taste the fruit of the trees planted by the revolution. They want to do so in peace and quiet, and "in safety," as the phrase was in 1789, without being dragooned by their superiors or subject to police supervision. The desire for freedom is inseparable from the desire for material prosperity. They want to travel beyond their own frontiers, to see foreign countries and study their achievements; they want to express their own opinions, to say what they think, to discuss the official attitudes and get to know different points of view.*

---

* Duverger, *op. cit.*, p. 368. I apologize to my colleague for quoting him so often, but when he allows his pen to run away with him no one reflects fashionable half-truths better.

I too believe that industrialization inevitably awakens a desire for material prosperity. I also think it probable that this desire in turn awakens a longing for certain kinds of freedom, just as I think it improbable that there could be a relapse into the frenzied excesses of Stalinism. (The example of Hitler's Germany should make us cautious in our forecasts, however. The Germans were a cultured people when they gave their support and faith to a demagogue, a barbaric monster endowed with a kind of political genius. Large societies organized on a democratic basis, but with no respect for tradition, are subject, perhaps, to bouts of feverish excitement and hysteria which give any political adventurer who happens to come along an opportunity to seize power.)

If I had to bet on the future, I would say that the odds are that in twenty-five or fifty years' time the Soviet Union will be Khrushchevian rather than Stalinist,* even more Khrushchevian than it is now. As the Revolution recedes into the past, revisionism gains ground, along with a more middle-class mode of life. The more men enjoy possession of a world they are in danger of losing, the less impatient they are to change that world. Beyond this banal fact, which is disappointing for idealists and reassuring for the conservatively minded, loom the real uncertainties.

At the present moment, peaceful co-existence is forbidden in the Soviet Union on the ideological level. In other words, Marxist-Leninist ideology retains the everlasting monopoly bestowed on it by the one-party system. But the continuation of the monopoly by no means excludes certain changes all of

---

* I wrote this before Khrushchev's downfall, but I am leaving the sentence unaltered. Khrushchev was a symbol. What he stood for did not necessarily disappear with him.

which may be listed under the heading of "liberalization." Marxism-Leninism did not demand that genetics or the theory of relativity be banned (such a ban being contrary to the interests of biology or physics and consequently to the interests of the state itself). It does not require the condemnation of formalism in art, and the rigors of socialist realism have, therefore, been considerably mitigated. At most, the party must abide by the principle that all intellectual activity, scientific as well as artistic, should be subject to its directives. Since it represents the proletariat and is building the future, the party has the right—or more accurately the duty—to see that all the members of the community work for the cause of socialism, especially intellectuals, who tend toward bourgeois individualism. It is true that both state and party leaders have acknowledged that the socialist state cannot do without scientists and that the latter must have absolute freedom in the laboratory. They have even accepted the fact that artists and writers need a certain degree of (supervised) freedom, but this must not exceed the limits imposed by the truth of the state ideology.

In other words, as soon as the single concept of freedom (which can be defined only by reference to a particular philosophy) is replaced by the concept of various forms of freedom, the equation freedom = material well-being loses its misleadingly obvious air. The right to visit foreign countries does not imply the right openly to question the truth of Marxism-Leninism. All communities, whether in obedience to the state or to the power of public opinion, in fact refrain from criticizing certain values or ideas. There is no evidence to support the view that the present trend toward liberalization in the East is leading spontaneously and of its own accord to all those forms of freedom to which we are accustomed in the West. It is obviously difficult to decide exactly how much liberty to allow.

The leaders know better than anyone that the margin between dogmatism and revisionism is narrow, and that intellectuals are only too eager to cross the frontiers within which the authorities try to imprison them. In fact, the system suffers from an internal contradiction: it is incapable of avoiding the creation of an intelligentsia and at the same time incapable of granting that intelligentsia the freedom it wants.

In any case, there is no necessary evolution from freedom of discussion within the intelligentsia to what we in the West call political freedom, at least if the latter is taken to imply free elections and the existence of competing political parties. This brings us to the heart of the issue: supposing the technical-administrative substructures in both types of society became increasingly similar, supposing even that the Soviet planners abandoned the irrationality of centralized authoritarian planning of the Stalinist type and, in the absence of rational planning by electronic computers, instituted a form of market economy, would this inevitably bring the one-party system and the ideological monopoly to an end? I have no hesitation in giving a negative answer.

The currently fashionable bias toward the opposite viewpoint represents the final phase of popular Marxism.* Were this bias expressed in more explicit terms, it would be tantamount to the proposition that the political-ideological system of a community is, at least in modern times, a function of the degree of expansion attained by its productive forces. This argument would have it that democracy goes hand in hand with material prosperity, while totalitarianism, which is almost inevitable during the phase of rapid primary industrialization, cannot

* The point has been made by Zbigniew K. Brzezinski and Samuel P. Huntington, *Political Power: USA/USSR* (New York: Compass Books, 1964).

hold out against prosperity. Western countries too have a theory of self-destruction, but their theory applies to socialism (or, if you like, to the Soviet system) and not to capitalism (or to Western-type democracies).

On the economic level, I have simply assumed that the Communist planning technique, which goes back to the first five-year plans and is now unanimously held to be progressively less compatible with the complexities of advanced industrial development, will evolve in the direction of methods more in keeping with the concept of rationality as held by Western theorists. (I have furthermore ruled out the possibility that computers will be used to combine rationality in respect of final consumption with centralized authoritarian planning without the existence of a market.) But from this possible evolution I have not drawn any conclusion on the method by which resources and income will be distributed. A system based on collective ownership might accept individual options as a necessary element in economic calculations, without replacing the collective ideal by the ideal of individual well-being.

Still less on the politico-ideological level do the inevitable concessions made to the intelligentsia and to the desires of the masses imply that the Soviet system is on the verge of collapse and decay. As far as one can judge, the freedom that the Soviet citizen demands most passionately, and whose loss he would feel most keenly, is the one that Montesquieu called "security." The Soviet people have terrible memories of the Stalinist police and the concentration camps. Stalin's successors lose no opportunity to affirm that "socialist legality" will never again be violated. Next in order to the desire for security comes the desire for intellectual and personal freedom, which is openly voiced by the intelligentsia but is not peculiar to them. But in the Soviet Union at least, such liberal aspirations are not expressed overtly as a plea for democracy in the sense of a system with a number of political parties, free elections, and the consequent right to challenge both the politicians and the system.

In a single-party system, any demand of this nature is automatically repressed and must remain underground as long as circumstances prevent it being openly expressed. In Hungary, it took the rebels no more than a day or two to move from liberalization, the initial aim of the uprising, to a multi-party system, which the Russian tanks had to be called in to prevent. This kind of rapid transition at a time of political crisis from a desire for liberalization to a demand for democracy is not impossible in the Soviet Union itself. On the other hand, it seems obvious that, so long as the party is not rent by internal quarrels, the Russian leaders are in a position to satisfy liberal aspirations, at least partially, without affecting the party's monopoly in any way.

Three main objections can be levelled against the theory that, in the industrial age, the one-party system is self-destroying under the influence of material prosperity.

The first can be drawn quite simply from the example of the West: Why should the development of productive forces and a rising standard of living have exactly the opposite effect in the East to that attributed to it in the West? Observers are delighted to point out that Marxist forecasts concerning the future of capitalist systems have been finally proved wrong, and this has been for a very simple reason: industrialization itself, especially in a society based on private ownership, gives an increasing number of people something to defend; instead of spreading poverty, it swells the ranks of the middle classes and ensures a lower-middle-class standard of living for a growing fraction of the total population. It is true that poverty alone does not create revolution, and ever since Tocqueville it has been repeated over and over that people become revolutionary only when their condition improves—or, to put it another way, when they can look to the future and gauge the distance between their present condition and the condition to which they are entitled or believe to be within their reach. But, the essential feature of industrialization today is not only that it ensures a gradual improvement of living conditions for the greatest number but that it also arouses a hope that the improvement will continue within the existing social framework. This is exactly what is happening in the Soviet Union. Pauperization no longer exists under either capitalism or socialism. Why should the masses not give their spontaneous support to a system which they believe to be responsible for their higher standard of living?

A second argument can be drawn from Western experience. Indifference to ideological distinctions, which people claim to observe in wealthy countries, will, in a single-party system, operate in favor of the party. If, in industrial societies, everything boils down to discussions about technology and profits (e.g., the balance to be struck between investment and consumption, and the distribution of income among the various classes), these discussions can take place more or less openly within a single-party system without interfering with the party monopoly. If "de-ideologization" actually takes place, it will strengthen conservative tendencies (in favor of the socialist system on the one hand, and the capitalist democratic one on the other).

The third and most powerful argument can be presented in

two forms, one theoretical, the other historical. Let us consider the theoretic ideal-type of industrialized society: it is characterized by specialization, by the determination of social function according to ability, by the diversification of industrial and individual activities, but above all by the *automization* of those stable entities which persist from one generation to the next and which are called classes. A fully developed society involves a complex stratification without necessarily being divided into classes that are consciously entities. In the light of this analysis, the single-party system can be seen as an ideally-typical solution to the problem of administration in industrialized societies that conform to democratic principles, are run by men of ability, but are lacking in political personnel chosen because of their social position or their ability. (Political talent is different from other forms of ability; it is not a result of education, and it cannot be gauged either by university degrees or competitive examinations.) The single party justifies its monopoly by its historical function—the building of the socialist state. It so happens that, in the present age at least, industrialized society seems to live in the future, whereas earlier societies wanted to live in the present or the past. Industrialized societies are eager to forecast the future, and they imagine that this future will be different from anything known before; pre-industrial societies tried to reduce the unforeseeable element of the future by imagining it to be similar to the past, or by thinking of it as part of a historical cycle. A party that defines itself by its dedication to building a future that is at once unprecedented and yet known in outline through the state ideology is not without some affinity with the spirit of modern civilization.

Expressed in historical terms, the same argument could be

advanced in the following simplified form. A political system does not automatically result from a given technical-administrative substructure: it is the product of a large number of forces and especially of the working of history. Soviet industrialized society was built by a state that took its inspiration from the Marxist-Leninist party; American society developed spontaneously, and until the time of the great depression the state did not play a major role in the processes of modernization and industrialization. If we express the contrast between the two systems in the most extreme terms, we can say that Soviet society springs ultimately from the state, whereas the American state springs ultimately from society*—a restatement, in a modified form, of the celebrated antithesis formulated by Tocqueville at the end of the first volume of *Democracy in America.* Pressure groups and political parties compete throughout the United States and constantly influence Congress and the Executive Branch (i.e., both politicians and civil servants). The Marxist-Leninist party does not permit the formation of pressure groups or parties, and it allows the trade unions as little initiative as possible. The Soviet Union has evolved toward an élitist structure which, while politically authoritarian, does not exclude a certain liberalism with regard to intellectuals, technicians, and even the *apparatchiki.* The United States has evolved toward a pluralist structure, with the reservation that a sufficient degree of conformism must be maintained within society and the authority of the federal government must be extended and strengthened. Each of the two countries is free to evolve without breaking with its own tradition or modifying its essential characteristics.

This brief analysis is merely intended to refute certain as-

* See Brzezinski and Huntington, *op. cit.*

sumptions about Soviet and American life that underlie various dogmatic forecasts. A high standard of living does not imply a democratic system in the Western sense, any more than a low standard of living excludes it (cf. India). But although such dogmatic assertions are not borne out by experience, it would also be a mistake to suppose that the evolution of the Soviet Union and the United States must inevitably follow the course I have just outlined. I can distinguish two main reasons for uncertainty on this score.

Every political system is an artificial and fragile structure. The American system insists on respect for the work of the founding fathers and on acceptance of practices that are contrary to technological rationality but that tradition decrees must not be changed; it calls for obedience to law and for moderation in political life, although both principles are constantly jeopardized by the violence of conflicts and political extremism. The transition from democracy to demagogy, which the Greek philosophers were fond of describing, is not inevitable, but democracy can never be sure of survival since it represents an ever-precarious compromise between consensus and the free expression of opinions and interests. Furthermore, chance events such as war, racial or economic crises, or a high-powered demagogue, can change the course of political development and leave a lasting if not ineradicable mark.

In the Soviet Union too, the system is self-contradictory. It has to allow the intelligentsia freedom of discussion and yet withhold the right to subject the state ideology to critical analysis. Economists must search for the most effective methods of planning the economy without infringing on Marxist dogma about historical development. Sociologists must study the workers' response to mechanization, automation, and even industrial discipline, but neither the sociologists nor the economists are permitted to query the fundamental principles of Marxism-Leninism or the identification of the party with the proletariat. The delegation of the proletariat's authority to the party is held to be permanent and final. Science and reason must not overstep the boundary that a so-called scientific doctrine guards. Here too, it is easy to imagine revisionists sweeping away the barriers, or party leaders losing control of events as a result of some succession crisis. It is true that, thanks to the progress already achieved, the party need never again subject the nation to the sacrifices and ordeals it demanded of the people between 1930 and 1953; it is equally true that an appetite for material prosperity and freedom is not easily thwarted and that sometimes it becomes keener after initial gratification.

The partial borrowings that in all probability each system will make from the other, particularly in the economic field, do not signify an inevitable common end in a kind of democratic socialism. Industrial society has no inherent finality. The ideological dialogue between the Soviet Union and the West will differ in the future from what it has been since 1917 and from what it is now. There is nothing to lead one to suppose that it will come to an end in the immediate future for lack of participants.

III

So-called *scientific Marxism* is first and foremost a *science of capitalism*. This fact has not always been fully understood. Marx, who was inexhaustible when describing or railing against capitalism, was always brief and allusive in his references to socialism. Moreover, like all his contemporaries, he knew nothing of the problems of a planned economy. He had chosen an objective theory of value, tempered by a distinction between values and prices that was philosophical rather than scientific (although he did not think so). The major difficulties of centralized planning, the fixing of objectives without recourse to economic prognosis, or economic prognosis without a market basis, were never even glimpsed in his system. Moreover, he was influenced by a residue of Hegelian thought—that man is free and creates an unforeseeable future—although the Marxist formula that the future is unforeseeable but will undoubtedly be socialist has always struck me as a contradictory, rather than a dialectical, proposition. (At least, it contains an unsurmounted contradiction.)

Be that as it may, Marxism was, until the Russian Revolution and the assumption of power in 1917, essentially a critical analysis—or a philosophically critical interpretation—of capitalism, and at once an economic and humanist (existentialist, to use the modern term) criticism. It denounced "capitalist anarchy" and the conditions that capitalism imposed on mankind, especially on the workers but also, in a more subtle way, on the employers themselves. On the level of propaganda if not of scientific accuracy, the effectiveness and apparent truth of Marxism were dependent on the evolution of capitalism. If capitalism continued to function and working-class living standards continued to rise, the principles that the militant Marxist, if not the theoretician, considered to be essential—pauperization, concentration, and self-destruction—would begin to appear doubtful. The first revisionist movement of the twentieth century, started by Eduard Bernstein, originated in the wave of capitalist prosperity that began during the last years of the nineteenth century and lasted until the First World War.

After the Marxists came to power in Russia, the dialogue

became at once more complex, more interesting, and more confused. Western economists, even those who were pessimistic about the working of the market economy, had all become aware of the central problem of a state planning system: how could the state ensure a rational distribution of resources if it had no price index at its disposal (i.e., no index of market prices showing the relative scarcity of goods; cost prices can, if necessary, be formulated in terms of raw materials and wages)? The result was that a genuine dialogue developed, especially after 1930, which involved criticism of the Soviet system by Western economists in addition to criticism of capitalism by Marxists.

This dialogue took place on two levels, involving two sets of questions: Which is the more efficient, economically, the Soviet system or the Western one? What are the political, social, and intellectual effects of each? For a long time, it was fashionable to claim superiority for the Soviet planning system in spite of its enormous human costs (the sacrifices of all forms of personal freedom). During the 1930's, there was a glaring contrast between the great depression and Russia's first five-year plans, but during the same period millions of Kulaks were deported and later the great purge wrought its havoc. The horrors perpetrated in the Soviet Union were partly camouflaged, it is true, by the most astonishing propaganda machine history has ever known, while Fascism and National Socialism, emerging at the same time, seemed to left-wing intellectuals the more urgent threat. The Soviet Union benefited from Hitler's outspoken hatred and from the progressives' hatred of him.

After 1945, the Soviet challenge took on its present proportions. The Soviet Union had emerged victorious from the war against the Third Reich; in the space of a few years, it had rebuilt its devastated cities; it dominated half of Europe; it could produce atomic and thermonuclear bombs; and it could boast a hitherto unprecedented rate of growth. The Western nations, which for the most part had viewed the Soviet experiment in planning with skepticism, could hardly fall back on some idealistic justification for this turn of events without being false to their own ideals or laying themselves open to ironic comment. If the Soviets had indeed discovered the secret of bigger and better productivity, even the argument that this achievement was counterbalanced by the enslavement of individuals and of the human mind would not have been strong enough to convince all the waverers. The Western nations had to face the test on ground chosen by the enemy, since productivity was becoming the gospel of the age, due to the return to Saint-Simonianism after the long interlude of Marxism.

However, one may wonder if the ground actually was chosen by the Marxist-Leninists. It is not certain that they based their claim to superiority on a higher growth rate. Western economists were as responsible as the Soviet economists (if not more so) for restricting the historic rivalry between East and West to one over growth rates. It is generally accepted, of course, that during the 1950's the rate of growth of the Soviet economy, even according to Western reckoning, was very high, higher than that of the American economy in particular and of capitalist economies generally (with the notable exception of Japan's). Yet, in the last analysis, the practice of attaching supreme importance to the growth rate is acceptable neither to Marxists nor to liberal democrats. The former are trying to build socialism, and the achievement of plenty through increased production is only a means to that end. The latter have no incentive to sacrifice the present generation to those of the future once the initial process of industrialization has been completed and the phase of self-sustained growth has been reached.

As a matter of fact, comparison of growth rates has become less fashionable since it no longer redounds to the glory of the Soviet system. The inadequacy of Soviet agriculture, the stagnation or even decline in industrial production in certain countries of Eastern Europe (e.g., Czechoslovakia), and the failure of the Great Leap Forward in China have prompted both Communist and Western commentators to adopt a more prudent attitude. It is wrong to draw confident conclusions from growth rates that depend (or may depend) on temporary circumstances. Why should Western nations set out to maximize their growth rates if their aim is to ensure the people's welfare and not the power of the state? The fact that growth is obtained by a high percentage of investment is no proof of the superior efficiency of the system, since the rate of growth will automatically fall the day people no longer produce in order to provide themselves with the means of producing more, and instead produce in order to satisfy the needs of the living. Perhaps inferior quality and minimal variety in consumer goods are the necessary accompaniment of rapid growth.

Actually, the significance attributed to economic expansion has not been the same in the East and the West. The Soviets, starting from the objective theory of value, took increased productivity as virtually their sole aim and tried to ignore consumer demands for anything that was not judged indispensable. Consequently, even as late as 1953, economists continued to be impressed by the growth rate while visitors were struck by the low standard of living. Soviet planners, obsessed by the determination to produce at whatever cost and to produce the greatest possible quantity of goods, continued to look beyond this to the kind of socialism Marx dreamed of, to the new society, cleansed of the taint of capitalism. In fact, production had become an absolute, and the socialist utopia a facile justification. Between the quantitative measurement of present production and the ultimate objective of socialism, the normal intermediary process, the raising of the living standard, was absent.

The opposite was equally true in the West. Starting from a subjective theory of value and imbued with the doctrines of the welfare state, Western nations did not distinguish between the growth of production and the welfare of the greatest number. Political leaders did not have sufficient power to ignore, even temporarily, the claims of the masses and to sacrifice consumption to investment. Nor did they possess the ideological means to transform the making of steel into a process ensuring the salvation of humanity. They tried to produce for public consumption, but this did not involve any promise as regards the creation of a new society.

As we have seen, the situation is now being reversed, since Khrushchevian revisionism is in a fair way to discover the virtues of the welfare state while at the same time playing down the traditional utopia. Henceforth, the satisfaction of consumer needs will take its place alongside the achievement of a given volume of production among the objectives of a planned economy. Concern with consumption and concern about the rational distribution of resources go hand in hand, since rationality demands economic calculation, which demands prices, and prices are determined by consumers' preferences. Can we say that the Soviet concept of plenty differs from the capitalist one? Growth is by definition a means to an end. Is the end the same in both camps, and will the final outcomes be similar?

The Soviets have not necessarily abandoned their socialist objective simply because they have acknowledged that man produces in order to consume, and not in order to go on producing more instruments of production. Consumption is not an absolute either. And the Western nations, too, are asking themselves what the aim of growth should be. It was unreasonable to turn the maximization of the growth rate into an unconditional criterion, as if economic development were a race in which present-day generations were supposed to toil and moil so that future generations (which, exactly?) might attain the desired objective (what objective?). Western nations are now pausing to reconsider the aim of material prosperity which they have pursued more or less consciously; they are wondering if the maximization of any particular kind of consumption is any better a criterion than the maximization of growth rates.

In part at least, the dialogue between the two systems has been an historic dialogue. Each system has influenced the development of the other. Neither Western opulence nor Chinese poverty was the only reason why Khrushchev attributed more importance to consumption; reason and the logic of industrialization prompted him to take this course. Also, the controversy between the two Europes on the question of the standard of living was in the long run bound to become intolerable for the socialist countries of the East, since they were forced to impose privations while at the same time proclaiming their faith in a philosophy of abundance. For their part, the Western nations might not have had the same awareness of the fundamental phenomenon of growth and might not have been so eager to adopt middle-term programming techniques and indicative planning if these techniques had not taken on the significance of a creative response to the Soviet challenge.

Is this tantamount to saying that the dialogue is moving toward an agreement, and that the dialectics of give and take, of hostility and imitation, will terminate in a peaceful conclusion? We have just seen, from the argument developed in the preceding pages, that there is no likelihood of this in present circumstances. Nor is it certain or likely in the immediate future. The Communist Party does not accept any limitation of its power as regards ideology (it and it alone fixes by law what the tenets of Marxism-Leninism are to be) or the economy (it and it alone determines the relative proportions of investment and consumption and decides whether to promote certain products or certain social groups at the expense of others) or policy (it is the agency through which the recruitment of political leaders is carried out). The political personnel of the country is identical with that of the party or, more probably, with the upper stratum of the party.

At the present time, the dialogue between the Soviet Union and the West is pursued on four different levels. The long-standing argument continues on the subject of the respective merits and demerits of market economies and centralized planned economies. On the propaganda level, Soviet spokesmen go on uttering their customary denunciations of capitalist monopolies or imperialism, although no event of contemporary history confirms the thesis of the self-destructive nature of capitalism; the fluctuations within the Western systems are becoming less pronounced, and rates of growth have been higher since 1945 than they were during the nineteenth century. The drop in East European rates of growth strengthens the Western cause still further. If one is considering the question only in the light of production and consumption, it might well be asked why Western nations should agree to sacrifice their liberties for the sake of a doubtful increase in the rate of growth.

On a somewhat higher level, the Western nations and the Soviet Union argue about the socio-political, that is, human, results attributable to their respective systems. They compare the degree of social mobility characteristic of each. They debate which of the two creates the better society and allows the worker to participate most effectively in industry and the citizen in the community. On this second, higher plane, we are no longer concerned with gauging the relative efficiency of means used to achieve unanimously accepted ends; we are comparing moral preferences and contrasting ideas about the good society. Even if we suppose that social mobility is greater under a Soviet-type regime than under a Western one, it is still unproved that the greater a society's mobility, the closer it approximates to the ideal. Of course, if you adopt the principle that all children should begin at the very same starting-point and that the offspring of the privileged should enjoy no advantage, a high coefficient of upward social mobility would at least be a favorable sign. But the radical elimination of continuity in social conditions from one generation to the next runs counter to the conservative ideal; and undogmatic sociologists would probably agree that this discontinuity has drawbacks. In any case, the complete elimination of continuity will be impossible in the foreseeable future: as long as variations in modes of family life continue, scholastic achievement, which is the first stage in the process of social selection, will reflect the child's environment as much as his inherited ability. It is in the interest of every society to see that it makes the most of exceptionally talented individuals; it is a matter of little importance, from the point of view of social utility, whether the average children of the privileged classes receive more or less favorable treatment. (They will inevitably be favored in any case.)

On a third level, we find a contrast between two versions of historical development, both of which could be said to be Marxist. There is the amended Marxist pattern of the succession of types of society, and the Clark-Rostow pattern of stages in economic growth (which also exists in the much cruder version of the "convergence theory," put forward, for instance, by Duverger). Marxist-Leninists in France rightly condemn the theory according to which the forces of production (sometimes referred to as the technological apparatus) are enough to determine the economic or political nature of a given society. Must we speak of a "revolution" every time a new source of energy is introduced? (If so, we should have to distinguish a steam age, an age of electricity, and an atomic age.) Is the advent of automation enough to mark the beginning of a new era? Two separate societies using atomic power and computers are not necessarily organized on the same principles. Nothing in Marx, except perhaps a few isolated sentences, or in the writings of Marxists in general, suggests the acceptance of such a simple causal explanation. Even if one uses the level of development in productive forces as it can be gauged by the amount produced by each worker instead of production technique, definition of a society on the basis of its national output or living standard remains at best an assumption, and more probably a question-mark.

Although it is easy to criticize a certain kind of evolutionary philosophy that Western nations have put forward in opposition to Marxist evolutionist philosophy, the task of Soviet theorists, who must be careful to interpret contemporary history in terms of orthodox principles, is much more difficult than that of their opposite numbers in Europe or the United States. Marxist-Leninists have no difficulty in refuting the determinist version of Western evolutionism, according to which a specific economic-political system *necessarily* corresponds to each stage of socio-economic development, or which maintains that Soviet socialism and Western capitalism will *necessarily* converge in a kind of democratic socialism. But Rostow himself is careful to avoid a categoric affirmation that a system can be defined by its phase of growth. Indeed, the Western theorist is in no way obliged to go beyond what I may call probabilist evolutionism, according to which each stage in growth is *conducive* to the establishment of a certain kind of system: viz., Sovietization is more likely to occur during the "take-off" stage than in an already industrialized society (barring accidents, such as a political crisis, war, or external pressure); the raising of technical standards and of the living standard reduces the danger of extreme forms of Stalinism and spreads a desire for freedom. Provided that the "objectivizing" method and the uncertainty of causal relations have been accepted, statements such as these are not open to the criticism that has been rightly directed against determinist evolutionism. But they are of only limited significance; however valid such analytical relations may be, a society in the end can be understood only in its unified totality. Yet Western theorists can go further in slackening the line of uncertain causality. Even if they begin at the same point—the universal process of industrialization—they may deny that at any given stage a country will inevitably adopt one system. If we compare the industrialization of Great Britain in the nineteenth century, of Japan since the last third of the nineteenth century, of the United States and the Soviet

Union, the differences between the political and intellectual systems—and, in some respects, between economic systems—are at least as striking as any resemblance. From this point of view, a society is defined as industrial according to the means of production it accumulates: this does not imply that it is necessarily oriented to any intricate or immanent end.

Soviet doctrinaire theorists, on the other hand, have to reconcile three propositions: that the Soviet Union will "catch up" with the United States in production and productivity (America is, therefore, acknowledged to be in the lead in this respect, in spite of its monopolistic capitalism); that the Soviet Union, a socialist state, has the most democratic system in the world and that there is therefore no parallel between the stages of economic growth and the succession of various types of government; that it is in the interests of underdeveloped countries to follow the noncapitalist path of development and, if possible, to take the Soviet Union as their model although they may develop even if they are not converted to Marxism-Leninism.

In debating with Western theorists, both French and Russian Marxist-Leninists attach more importance to *production relationships,* which include classes and class conflicts, than to *forces of production,* which are stressed by Western specialists who refer to them as stages of growth and gauge them according to the national product. Marxist-Leninists must therefore begin by refuting the Western theory according to which Soviet practices can be held to have some justification during the "take-off" stage but none at all in a fully developed economy; next, they must prove that a Soviet system, reduced to its essential features and purged of any trace of the personality cult, is intrinsically superior to the capitalist systems of the West, either from the point of view of economic efficiency or as regards human values.

This brings us to the fourth level on which the dialogue is taking place. The two kinds of industrial society are both trying to produce as much as possible—one with the purpose of building socialism, the other with the purpose of spreading material prosperity or raising the standard of living. One has rediscovered that you cannot build socialism if you fail to satisfy men's needs. The other is beginning to recover from its obsession with productivity and to do some soul-searching about what it is aiming at over and above production and opulence. Both have arrived, not at the same point of development, but at the same query: What is the final purpose—in the double sense of objective and ultimate value—of industrial societies? Or, more accurately, what purpose will men give them?

The weakening of Stalinist dogmatism and social change in both East and West have given the continuing debate between Soviet and Western theorists fresh life. In Stalin's time, Western observers criticized the new faith by insisting, as Milosz said, on the discrepancy between the doctrine and the reality. In those days, I argued with progressives, not with Marxist-Leninists, because no worth-while exchange of views was possible with the latter. Since 1953, the Marxist-Leninists have again begun discussions amongst themselves and with us. As a result, instead of a futile clash of total systems, impervious to experience and reason, we have again—beyond the controversy over the relative efficiency of differing systems—the eternal problems of political thought.

Ideological dogmatism had to disappear before ideas could live again.

DEAD IDEOLOGIES, LIVING IDEAS

The end of ideologies has been a fashionable theme for the past ten years.* Today, I am pleased to note, it is criticized not only by Marxist-Leninists, as it always was, but also by radicals (in the American sense of the term) and ex- or semi-Marxists. Consider as evidence two articles, both published in *Commentary*—one in April, 1964, by Henry David Aiken, entitled "The Revolt against Ideology," the other in June, 1964, by George Lichtheim, entitled "The Cold War in Perspective."

Aiken launches a simultaneous, systematic attack on Camus, myself, Daniel Bell, and other American professors. Not surprisingly, he finally discovers that "it is virtually impossible to argue with them without fear of doing them some frightful injustice." It would have been better to avoid the risk and to have refrained from creating a fictitious school of "anti-ideologists" by bracketing together Camus, myself, European opponents of Marxism, and American sociologists or pragmatists. What we have in common is our opposition to Marx-

* In a work of my own entitled *The End of the Ideological Age?*, I made this comment: "We are not, of course, so naïve as to expect peace in the immediate future: the conquerors having been disappointed or liquidated, the bureaucrats continue to reign. The peoples of the West may dream of political tolerance, just as three centuries ago they tired of futile slaughter perpetrated on both sides in the name of the same God for the choice of the true Church. But they have infected the rest of the world with their faith in a radiant future. Nowhere, in Asia or in Africa, has the welfare state as yet spread enough benefits to stifle the impulse of unreasonable hope."

Edward Shils used the expression "The End of Ideology" for the title of a report on a meeting of the Congress for Cultural Freedom in Milan in 1955. Daniel Bell gave the same title to a collection of his essays. And Seymour Martin Lipset published a bibliography of books and articles dealing with the subject.

ism-Leninism and to the type of ideology of which it is the perfect embodiment. But our opposition does not necessarily spring from the same source. Kantians or pragmatists are also anti-ideologists, but the meaning of their "revolt against ideology" is obviously not the same.

Furthermore, in any debate worthy of the name, there should be no playing on words, particularly on a word as ambiguous as "ideology." It is well known that Marxism too was originally a revolt against ideology, ideology sometimes being taken to mean a false awareness, or a biased distortion, of reality and sometimes as a whole complex of intellectual and moral structures. Whether in the broad or narrow sense, the Marxist-Leninists glibly "unmasked" it, as if their own ideas could not as easily be subject to the same treatment. They looked upon their own system as having the dignity of a science of history in contrast to idealist illusions, as a total vision in contrast to individual opinions, as a form of thought oriented to the future through hope as opposed to ideas fossilized in conservatism through fear of the unknown.

In my view, Stalinism was the extreme, grotesque form of what I called an ideology, that is, *a pseudo-systematic formulation of a total vision of the historical world,* a vision that gave meaning both to the past and to the present, that deduced what ought to be from what is, and that forecast the desired future which was to emerge from present reality. Under the name of ideology, I criticized what I have elsewhere called a *secular religion.** There is no trace of ideology in this sense in the final passage of *The Opium of the Intellectuals:* "If tolerance

* During the war, in 1943, I wrote a study of secular religions, of which national socialism was at the time the most striking and monstrous example.

is born of doubt, then let us teach everyone to doubt model societies and utopias, to challenge all the prophets of redemption and the heralds of catastrophes. If they alone can abolish fanaticism, let us pray for the advent of the skeptics." Aiken, however, comments, "The rhetoric is appealing. But it smacks of ideology, in Aron's own sense. For tolerance is also a principle and a method. And it too has its dangers." This kind of polemical argument, advanced by a professor of philosophy at Harvard University, would have surprised me were I still capable of surprise in such matters. If my skepticism were applied to all "principles" and all "methods," it would obviously destroy any possibility of reasonable decisions or action. For any fair-minded reader of *The Opium of the Intellectuals,* it was clear that my skepticism was directed against "models and utopias," i.e., against the ideal market, cherished by liberals, and against total planning, cherished by socialists. I was attacking the "prophets of redemption and the heralds of catastrophe," all those who look upon the extermination of millions of men as the first step to redemption.

The Opium of the Intellectuals, which was basically a negative book, was directed in the first place at the Marxist-Leninists, even more precisely at progressives. In dealing with an intelligentsia that had excommunicated me because I denounced Stalinism and supported the Atlantic Alliance, I felt no need to examine the basis of those values to which I subscribed, as did the progressives; I was arguing neither with fascists nor with reactionaries but with the Left—that is, with the spiritual family I had sprung from and which I was accusing of betrayal. Neither Camus nor myself had any feeling that we had changed sides; we were denouncing the usurpers, since Stalinism had set itself up as the inheritor of the tradition of the Enlightenment. Against a political system deriving from a philosophy of history, we put forward a political system guided by empirical knowledge and animated by a moral purpose.

Apart from these intentional or unintentional misunderstandings, the criticism leveled against the "revolt against ideology" nonetheless poses one or two problems worthy of close study. Reduced to their essential points, they would seem to be as follows:

1. The theory that the ideological age is coming to an end is first and foremost a diagnosis of the historical situation. For this reason, considered as a statement of fact, it requires either confirmation or refutation on that level. In short, the first question concerns the truth or falsity of the analysis, or if you like, its degree of truthfulness or falsehood.

2. Supposing the analysis to be accurate, should the end of the ideological age be welcomed or deplored? More generally, what are the existing or probable consequences of political thought that is, or tries to be, nonideological?

3. What philosophy, what vision of the world, is held by those who proclaim this hostility to ideologies? Does the end of ideologies signify the decline or the revival of political philosophy?

I

The analysis of the historical situation in the West ran roughly as follows: the last world war discredited ideologies of the Fascist or National Socialist type which extolled one particular nation or race and combined nostalgia for pre-industrial hierarchies with action and propaganda techniques imitated from the socialist and, more particularly, Communist parties.

Even conservatives or moderates in developed countries for the most part now favor economic expansion, industrialization, and rationalization. The dialogue is now, essentially, between the two versions of rationalist thought, the Western and the Soviet. Now Western-type liberal democracy, once it ensures the development of the productive forces and the spread of material prosperity, possesses an obvious superiority (except in the eyes of certain intellectuals) over the so-called popular democracy of the Soviet type. What good is the single-party system or the totalitarian state if, in fact, the liberal democracies obtain at least as good economic results amid the disorder and debates of freedom? In 1954–55, I felt that the mist concealing Soviet reality was lifting; I thought that faith in Marxism-Leninism would be at least shaken by the discovery of this reality, and I could see no other ideology that might take its place.

Why is it so difficult to evolve an ideology, in the sense of a total system of interpretation and action? For contemporary societies, scientific and technological progress has acquired a kind of inevitability, an almost irresistible movement that no government is willing either to halt or to slow down (the race for knowledge is also a race for power). Perhaps no government is able to harness it completely. (Perhaps they hope that one day man, through the discoveries of biological research, will be able to "control" his own heredity.) Progress in science and growth in production are inseparable, and taken together, they create a future the broad lines of which are foreseeable but which is unpredictable, in human terms, beyond the next ten or twenty years.

Beyond a certain point (here again I refer to advanced Western societies), neither knowledge nor economic growth are noticeably affected by any declared preferences of the party in power. The age-old problem of inequality is not "solved" (supposing it could ever be solved) simply by the advent of an affluent (or semi-affluent) society, but it does not present itself in the same terms once the collective resources show a yearly increase and the mass of the population benefits from this increase. Neither liberal rule (in the United States) or the rule of the Left (in Europe) necessarily increases or decreases the rate of growth, any more than either has a sustained effect in one direction or another on inequality of distribution.

How can we reconstruct a new ideology when so many components are missing: the culprit (private ownership or capitalism, which can be blamed for exploitation and poverty); the savior (the proletariat, which bears witness to the inhumanity of society and is destined for redemption); and the vision of a radiant future (the knowledge of what the prosperous society will be like provided economic progress is maintained at its present rate for another half century and no catastrophe occurs)? Social institutions and mechanisms no longer lend themselves easily to transplantation, since the existing systems are becoming less and less "pure" and borrow from ideal-types that, on the abstract level, are incompatible. Most important of all, the present trend of history illustrates both the power of technology when applied to the environment and the resistance of human nature and society to those whose ambition it is to "reconstruct" the social order. What is more, events seem to show that the more fervently men believe in the Promethean illusion that they are shaping history, the more readily they submit to it; on the other hand, leaders who modestly approach problems as they occur are more likely to obtain results that correspond to their intentions. The pragmatic approach of the social engineer, not the vast ambition of the ideologist, is most in keeping with the spirit of rationalism and gives men the best opportunity, not to become "masters and possessors of society," but to improve it while accepting its rules.

In Europe, no one any longer denies that "ideological syntheses" have lost their force. Observers of the European scene even tend to apply the term *depoliticization* to what is merely indifference to traditional ideologies. The French peasant who has become aware of the link between his earnings and the Common Market is, in a sense, more politicized, more fully integrated into the national and European complex than his father was, even though he sometimes votes on the Right, sometimes on the Left, according to circumstances and the programs of the candidates, whereas his father always voted Radical. The fact that politics are no longer identified with rivalries between spiritual families but are concerned with social and economic issues does not yet mean that the Frenchman has ceased to be a citizen; he is in the first place a citizen belonging to a community of workers. As Aiken himself admits: "No doubt the old ideologies of the right and the left have lost much of their power to persuade, and no doubt all over the world radicalism and intellectualism in our time must inevitably take new forms." In Germany, in England, and in Scandinavia, "pragmatic socialists" stand in opposition to "enlightened conservatives." In France and Italy, the Communist parties have kept their voters, their officials, and their militant wing; but having become less rigid ideologically, they no longer have the same power to charm or bewitch intellectuals.

It is worth asking whether the situation in the United States today is different from the analysis I gave ten years ago. The nomination of Barry Goldwater by the Republican Party and the appearance of books or articles directed against the "liberals" (Burnham's, for instance) are evidence of a renewed quarrel between the liberals (the American equivalent of the Left) and the conservatives. The moderate liberalism that prevails in the universities and in Washington is attacked on the Left by "radicals" or "para-Marxists" and on the Right by conservatives.

Anti-ideological attitudes of American writers from the outset differed in character from the anti-ideological attitude of someone like Camus, who had been a Communist in his youth, or like myself, who had never ceased to argue with the representatives of Hegelian-Marxist thought. In the United States, "liberalism" has been influenced by Marxism hardly at all; it has only rarely been formulated systematically or built up into a philosophy of history. After 1945, liberals were, with a few exceptions, resolutely anti-Communist. In America, there has been no equivalent of Burke-type conservatism, or Marxism à la Kautsky or Lenin, or even Sartrian progressive attitudes. The American belief in free enterprise has seldom found expression in a theoretical system in the style of Mises or Hayek. In moving away from ideology, the American anti-ideologists did not have far to go; some were merely relinquishing their ties with Europe; but more often than not, their change of attitude had a different significance. In Europe, anti-ideologists denounced a philosophy of history which had hardened into a kind of rigid, inhuman dogmatism and appealed to morality or wisdom; in the United States, the traditional dialogue was, rather, between moralism and pragmatism, between a political system founded on principles and one dictated by utilitarian considerations or empirical knowledge.*

* Since Aiken fails to make any distinction between the European dialogue (philosophy of history vs. moral purpose) and the American dialogue (principles vs. pragmatism), his study abounds in confused ideas.

Perhaps the arguments begun by both right- and left-wing intellectuals—Aiken, Lichtheim, Marcuse, Burnham—herald a new era of discussion. The election results of 1964 confirmed, were such confirmation necessary, that moderate liberalism, when in power, need fear no threat from the right or the left. What I refer to as moderate liberalism corresponds to what in French we prefer to call democratic-liberal orthodoxy. In fact, the political systems of the advanced Western nations today represent an acceptable compromise between the characteristic values of liberalism, democracy, and socialism. The fact that ideological quarrels in the West have become less intense (which all observers, including those most hostile to the idea of the "end of ideology," concede) is, as it happens, due to the present success of this compromise. Personal liberties are preserved, in spite of the increasing intervention of the state in the economic sphere, in spite of social legislation, and in spite of the subsidizing of agriculture. The parliamentary system and free elections do not prevent rapid economic growth; semi-planning is not inconsistent with representative institutions. Reactionaries and revolutionaries, Whigs and Marxists, launch ineffectual attacks against the bastions of the moderate left (or enlightened conservatism). The present holders of power in the United States, accused by some critics of paving the way for socialism and assailed by others for betraying the radical tradition of the left, are true interpreters of the feelings of the majority. Admittedly, the "liberal credo" as it finds expression today on both sides of the Atlantic owes more to nineteenth-century socialism than to eighteenth-century liberalism. It is less apprehensive of strengthened state power than of continued inequality or the power of capitalists or big corporations. In abstract terms, it is concerned more with equality than with freedom, in the eighteenth-century sense of individual liberty. Of those who subscribe to the same credo, some are prepared to sacrifice individual freedom to democracy (i.e., to a government representative of the popular will) while others attach more importance to individual liberty than to the method of electing leaders. As a matter of fact, most left-wing intellectuals in Europe are more socialist than liberal (in the European sense of the term), and it is this which makes them critical of things as they are: the distribution of wealth is far removed from the egalitarian ideal, and semi-planning is carried out with the cooperation of big corporations that are more secure today than they were thirty years ago.

I certainly do not claim that the present situation in the West is characteristic of the human political condition generally, or even characteristic of modern times: I am inclined to believe the opposite. Extreme situations are in many respects more typical, at least during those periods when history is, to use Toynbee's expression, in a "state of flux." The present situation in the West does not call for serious or immediate sacrifices in respect of freedom, democracy, or economic growth. There is disagreement about questions of degree; each party or individual has its or his own scale of values, each is more or less aware of the order in which it or he would sacrifice these values if sacrifices became inevitable.

Since there are no major quarrels within the societies to which they belong, Western intellectuals (excluding Marxist-Leninists) seek to nourish their dreams and indignation further afield.

"It is certainly true," writes Lichtheim, "that revolutionary passions have cooled in the West . . . and that something like a consensus is coming about in the most advanced countries. It is also true that Western conservatives have been unsuccessful in trying to impose their constipated outlook on people still struggling with the urgent problem of keeping alive. But it is emphatically *not* the case that the backward countries would do better if they adopted our own piecemeal approach. 'Social engineering' is no answer to their problem. A 'total interpretation of world history' is an urgent practical necessity for them if they are to break with the past and reshape their cultures; and until they do, they will make no material progress." This passage, which contains an element of truth, is an example of the kind of argument to which the half-repentant Marxist resorts. It urges the underdeveloped countries to follow the path of revolution and therefore to adopt an authoritarian, and probably totalitarian, regime (since a government "inspired by a total vision of history" claims to have the monopoly of truth). The official spokesmen of most underdeveloped countries put economic growth before democratic and liberal values, or at least they give the necessity of expansion as a justification of their power. But, in fact, Sukarno's Indonesia was more interested in extending its territory in New Guinea and Malaysia than it was in economic progress and the people's standard of living. Algeria and Morocco quarrel about their frontiers and Ben Bella's administration, although avowedly socialist, seemed to aim at power rather than material prosperity. Over a large area of the underdeveloped world, events would seem to prove that those peoples who, in the words of Lichtheim, are fighting for survival, prefer glory and ideas to life itself. To give absolute priority to development is much more characteristic of the European intellectual than it is of Asian or African ruling groups. It may be that India, which remains unaffected by secular religions and the "total vision of world history," and which respects traditional beliefs while at the same time aiming at modernization, has been, since becoming independent, one of the countries most deeply concerned with economic growth. It will most certainly be objected that the results in India have not been brilliant, and that respect for sacred cows or monkeys raises obstacles in the way of modernization which parliamentary democracy will take a long time to overcome. This I readily admit, but if the rejection of despotism and violence has its drawbacks, despotism and violence can also be costly in terms of sweat, blood, and tears, without bringing about development. Fidel Castro has a total vision of history, yet in the space of a few years he has managed to reduce sugar production, to fail to industrialize Cuba, and to find himself at loggerheads with the whole of the Western hemisphere. He did not want to be dependent on the United States; today, he is more dependent on Soviet aid than he ever was on his commercial relations with the neighboring continent. He has caused the departure of an important section of the middle classes—the teachers, doctors, and technicians who were indispensable for modernization. Truly, one must be a conservative with a "constipated outlook" not to admire such admirable achievements.

Can it be said that Indonesia, Ben Bella's Algeria, or Castro's Cuba lack a "total interpretation of world history" and that therein lies the chief cause of their failures? Or would not a keener sense of "social engineering" have permitted them to avoid the mistakes that "global visions" encourage, not to say provoke? In short, must it be agreed that only the Marxist-Leninist interpretation is both total and effective?

Let me make my point quite clear. I would not presume to dictate to the governments of so-called underdeveloped countries what priorities they should establish during the initial stages of industrialization among many often incompatible values. I do not deny that authoritarian regimes may be historically inevitable, or that they may be indispensable for the accomplishment of reform. But I object to revolutionary conformism being applied to underdeveloped countries by Western intellectuals who see no prospects of revolution in their own countries. Admittedly, modernization is always accompanied by hardship and demands a spiritual conversion; I agree that a global vision of history can facilitate the break from the past; but I cannot either advocate or condemn a violent breakaway, ideological despotism, or contempt for age-old beliefs (even those which may have the effect of slowing down modernization). There is greater diversity among those countries which are called underdeveloped than among those commonly supposed to be advanced; some, perhaps, are in need of a "global interpretation of history," but all need to be guided by the skill of the social engineer. National circumstances must be considered in determining the best method of procedure, although this method may not necessarily win the day. Castroism was the logical outcome of the passions of Castro himself and of a group of Cuban intellectuals; it was not the technique of development best suited to the situation.

Besides, when Lichtheim affirms that a total interpretation of history is necessary for underdeveloped countries, he is going back not so much to Marx as to Georges Sorel. Marx believed in the truth of his doctrine, but the author of *Réflexions sur la violence* justified myths by their social utility. Lichtheim does not even imply that he himself has a total interpretation of history. He does not stop to examine the truth of such an interpretation. Comfortably settled in either Great Britain or the United States, he is afraid lest the governments of the underdeveloped countries be won over to the "constipated outlook," to the narrow, humdrum vision of reality with which the Western peoples tend to be satisfied. In underdeveloped countries, where Western intellectuals do not live, the glorious visions that inspire glorious slaughter have retained their glamor. There is little in Western history that allows us to hope, or fear, that nations are capable of doing without revolutions. But if we compare the ways in which Great Britain and France evolved towards political democracy in the last century, we must have a lot of romanticism in our make-up to prefer the French to the British; and if the Bolshevik Revolution is considered as essentially a method of industrialization, we must have a lot of pessimism or shortsightedness not to see that another, less costly method might have been found.

With or without our approval, the developing countries will carry out their revolutions. Let us leave the new governing groups to shoulder the responsibility of the independence they have won without setting ourselves up as judges or lecturing to them about democracy or revolution. As a matter of fact, the leaders of newly created states have on the whole been only too prompt to learn the art of absolute power and to discover the indispensability of the scaffold. What is the use of strengthening their conviction that their executions are in accordance with the dictates of the historical process? The only effect would be to relieve them of all doubt or scruple.

II

Let us go back to the subject of the advanced countries, since they are the only ones to which the theory of the decline in

ideologies applies. Are we to deplore the fact that ideological
fervor has spent itself? Are the anti-ideologists spreading a
gospel of skepticism and conservatism? Are they urging us to
disregard necessary reforms and to turn a blind eye on the in-
adequacies or injustices of our societies?

The adherents of the school of thought which, for polemical
purposes, has been dubbed the "revolt against ideology" are
condemned in the following terms by Aiken:

> Were their political and social attitudes generally to prevail in
> the West—and it is primarily of the West that they speak in
> talking of the end of ideology—the result would be a pessimistic
> *carpe diem* philosophy which would render us helpless in the
> world struggle against the ideology of Communism. At home,
> in the political parties, in the Congress, and in the courts, it con-
> tinually weakens what remains of our national commitment to
> the ideological principles that animate our constitutional sys-
> tem: in the Presidency, it provides merely the covering excuses
> for a spate of uncorrelated, "piecemeal" moves which, however
> admirable from a tactical point of view and however skillful as
> "pragmatic" politics, result in an ever-increasing loss of basic
> political control and social direction.

The charge involves two items:

1. The anti-ideologists profess a pessimistic philosophy and
thereby discourage action and leave the West undefended
against Communism.

2. American policy, because it has no loyalty to principles,
is no more than a juxtaposition of individual measures; this
leads to the loss of basic political control.*

Let us consider, first, the allegation of pessimism and the
effect that pessimism might conceivably have. According to
Aiken, "like Camus and Popper, Aron cannot bring himself

* I am unable to give any precise meaning to expressions such as *basic
political control* or *social direction.*

flatly to renounce the values of the Enlightenment; but in practice, he is no more able than they to take them with absolute seriousness as governing ideals for the reconstruction of society in the twentieth century. In his own terms, he no longer fully believes in the vision of a future consistent with 'human aspirations.' And it is this fact perhaps that accounts for the vein of pessimism and the self-division which runs through his writing."

I do not know to what generation Aiken belongs, but any man living in the same century as Hitler and Stalin who does not experience from time to time some doubts about the temporal destiny of humanity, must be supported by what, on the kindest possible view, is a very naïve and simple faith. Millions of Jews were exterminated in the name of racism, millions of kulaks were deported for the purpose of agrarian collectivization, millions of innocent people were thrown into prison by a despot who was acclaimed by tens of thousands of intellectuals the world over, and if all these deaths and absurdities have not shaken my system of values, they have at least put me on guard forever against people who talk of "reconstructing society" (those strange builders who always begin by destroying) and have roused me from the dogmatic slumber induced by philosophies of history. I do not know what the future for humanity will be, but I do know that we do not know. Those who claim to know are deliberately falsifying the truth. We are entitled to hope for a future in keeping with human aspirations, but not to present our hope as a certainty, and still less to expect confidently that the laws of history or the action of one particular party (or class) will bring it about.

In addition to being prudent in this way, I am prepared to admit that in comparison with many "liberal" Americans and perhaps even more so with the French Left, I am justifiably thought to be a pessimist. I do not believe that it is an easy task to shape either human nature or human society. I am astonished that the same men who show no forbearance in judging their fellows should demand from society a perfection to which no individual existence can attain; I am astonished that the same men should appeal to reason and disregard the limitations of the certainties which reason offers us and, still more so, of its influence on the behavior of individuals and nations.

James Burnham, in his book *Suicide of the West,* claims that the American liberal credo can be summarized in nineteen propositions. Some of these express an optimism to which I certainly do not subscribe, for instance, the first: "Human nature is changing and plastic, with an indefinite potential for progressive development and no innate obstacle to the realization of the good society of peace, justice, freedom, and well-being." Or: "The obstacles to progress and the achievement of the good society are ignorance and faulty social institutions." Or once again: "Because of the extrinsic and remediable nature of the obstacles, it follows that there are solutions to every social problem and that progress and the good society can be achieved: historical optimism is justified."

I am not certain that the majority of American liberals or the French left wing would endorse such dogmatic affirmations. Personally, I would express myself in different terms. I do not believe there are immediate solutions to all social problems, or that all the obstacles to progress and the good society are extrinsic to man's nature. But I also do not believe that we can set limits in advance to the development of individuals and communities. Neither ignorance nor social institutions are the sole cause of the evils that afflict mankind, although individuals have no hope of realizing the best in themselves if they are raised in slums and deprived of a decent education.

Besides, it is of little importance to know whether a given person is more or less optimistic or pessimistic about the future of humanity. (Probably each of us inclines now to one side, now to the other.) The question is to know what inferences each individual draws from his attitude. Some optimists are inclined to inaction, some to violence; some pessimists are inclined to action, some to moderation. For the past twenty years, I have fought against fanatics who claim to be optimists but who are prepared to accept, or rather to justify, any crime provided it is committed in the name of the right ideas and by the party to which they have given their allegiance. My alleged pessimism has never prompted me to be either indifferent or passive. Far from weakening the defenses of the West against Communism, anti-ideology (its degree of optimism or pessimism is immaterial) provides it with the best possible protection.

Non-Communists will never succeed in elaborating a verbal system as coherent in its falsity as Marxism-Leninism, at once scientific and philosophical, pitiless and humanitarian, confident in both its identification of "criminals" and its forecast of ultimate reconciliation. The Communists are heirs to the Enlightenment (or to the European Left) in whom Hegelian dialectics and the vicissitudes of history have produced a kind of delirium (a logical delirium). Conservatives are not wrong when they point out the common inspiration behind liberals and communists, the external left and the internal left, the extreme left and the moderate left, Marxist-Leninists and social democrats. All claim to be rationalists, put their trust in science and reason, and reject passive acceptance of the age-old social order. The moderate left has taken over a number of socialist demands; it has moved away from the individualism of the Enlightenment and the *laissez-faire* approach of the nineteenth century. Nevertheless, on the political level, the two left-wing movements have become mortal enemies. (When Bolsheviks are in power, the Mensheviks' place is in prison.) On the intellectual level, too, they are rivals who can be reconciled only by conversion on the one side or apostasy on the other—the conversion of Communism to ideological coexistence, or the repudiation of liberal values by the moderate left.

In a dialogue of this kind, the moderate left cannot and must not appeal to the same type of ideology as that put forward by the Marxist-Leninists, first because it has no such ideology, and secondly because an ideology of this sort would divide those who are united in their response to a single threat and their common rejection of it. The moderate left is in fact, in the present circumstances, anti-ideological in a very precise and limited sense: in each particular situation it tries to reconcile in the best possible, or least unsatisfactory, way personal freedom, democratic legitimacy, economic progress, and the lessening of social inequalities. It is precisely because complete reconciliation is impossible except as a remote rational concept that the moderate left declares itself "anti-ideological" and stresses the diversity of political situations and the fragility of vast syntheses. It is because developed societies are at least partially succeeding in achieving such a reconciliation that they cannot or will not formulate an ideological synthesis.

What is more, the approximate reconciliation achieved by highly developed societies is more often than not out of the question for societies in the initial phases of modernization. What are we to deduce from "principles"? Should personal liberties be sacrificed to the speeding up of economic growth, or vice versa? Should despotism be accepted in the interests of modernization? Such questions admit of no final, universally valid answer. Being firmly rooted in history as it is, political action calls for philosophical reflection but cannot be deduced from principles.

Present-day societies do not present a single problem but a variety of problems and I must confess that I am unable to ascribe any reasonable meaning to Aiken's formula: "One of the fundamental principles of any declaration of the rights of man (such a declaration implies the carrying into effect of a set of ideological convictions) is that it reduces, in the most rigorous way possible, the number of problems about which men in society continue to wrangle." To begin with, the translation into action of any of the rights of man gives rise to endless controversy. The different rights are not all compatible. It is perhaps a good thing to impose nondiscrimination by law, but in so doing you deprive certain individuals of rights they thought were laid down in the preamble to the Constitution. Finally—and not least important—why should the task of philosophers be to imitate politicians and to replace the complexity of social problems by a few simple formulas, as if one had only to invoke the declaration of the rights of man to find the answers to all these questions raised by a society that is in many respects radically different from all societies previously known?

Is it true that those who claim or who are held, to be hostile to ideologies are more inclined to put up with compromise? Do they judge the injustices of Western society less strictly than they should? I am not sure, but if it is true, the connection is no more than a psychological link. In Western societies, to reject a total synthesis is not tantamount to making a profession of conservative faith, or accepting racial discrimination, or doubting the necessity for moral and sociological criticism of things as they are; it is simply to state that no one (apart from the Marxist-Leninists) conceives of a social order radically different from the established one. Our task is neither to maintain it exactly as it is nor to destroy it, but to improve it.*

I must admit that I am more than ever convinced that the very word "ideology" is full of ambiguities. A French sociologist has listed thirteen different meanings. The essential point is that in current practice writers oscillate between a pejorative, critical, or polemical use of the word (ideology is a mistaken concept, the justification of vested interests and passions) and a neutral use (ideology is the more or less rigorous formulation of an attitude toward social or political reality, a more or less systematic interpretation of what is or is not desirable). In a pinch, any philosophical discourse can be called ideological. When this happens, "ideology" becomes a laudatory, not a pejorative, term—meaning either the permanent expression of any thought worthy of the name of philosophy or a source of inspiration for effective action—and is proudly used to confute analysts, positivists, pragmatists, and conservatives.

* In a reply to Daniel Bell's reply (*Commentary,* October, 1964), Aiken gives nuclear disarmament and the recognition of Communist China as examples of the reforms he hopes for. I cannot see that anti-ideologists as such must be either for or against these two proposals, the first of which is unrealizable for the time being and the second of which will probably be achieved in the near future. As regards domestic policy, he demands radical measures in favor of the Negro minority and continues: "There is also the immense aesthetic and even religious problem of saving America and the world from total permanent disfigurement. . . . The countryside is in ruins. The air stinks." Proposals to improve the lot of the black minority appear in all the programs of the "liberal establishment"; as for saving nature and the countryside, it seems to me that the engineer would be more useful in this connection than the ideologist.

Ten years ago, I drew attention to certain historical phenomena the reality of which is admitted by those who are most critical of the anti-ideologists—namely, the dwindling of revolutionary passions and the existence of a kind of consensus of opinion in the developed countries. (I called this democratic-liberal conformism.) I referred to the whole development as "the end of the ideological age," since I explicitly defined ideology as *a total system of interpretation of the historic-political world.* It is still true, I think, that total systems, whether of liberals like Hayek, or of Marxists, are in decline, but it is not easy to distinguish between an ideology that is *the formulation of a historical attitude or scale of values* and therefore characteristic of all politics, at any rate of the democratic sort, and an ideology that is *a total system of interpretation,* which is what I have chosen to designate by the term "ideology." The ambiguity inherent in the concept inevitably colors the idea of an end to the ideological age.

Moreover, the analysis of the end of the ideological age implied a kind of eulogy of pragmatism and the belittling of total intellectual systems. I linked my analysis of a given situation with a value judgment, without stating exactly what significance I myself gave to that judgment. It might be wondered whether the skepticism I recommended with regard to "models and utopias" was related to the particular circumstances of the moment or to all circumstances in general. I have tried to deal with these points in the preceding pages.

In my view, criticism of ideologies was a necessary reaction of the early 1950's to the existential-Hegelian-Marxist frenzy of the years following the liberation. At the same time, beyond a certain stage in its development industrial society itself seems to me to widen the range of problems referable to scientific examination and calling for the skill of the social engineer. Even forms of ownership and methods of regulation, which were the subject of doctrinal or ideological controversies during the past century, seemed to me then (and still seem) to belong primarily to the realm of technology. The sanctification or transfiguration of economic and social ideal-types is contrary to sound reason and intellectual honesty. This is not to say that objective study can ever replace choice or that science dictates the form that truth is to take in practice; the effects of forms of ownership and methods of regulation are too numerous and too uncertain for us to assert that any one of them is to be preferred to another *in all respects.* But it would be ridiculous to replace methodical inquiry by an arbitrary assumption that would be ideological (in the pejorative sense) if it were not based on experience.

I am more aware today than I was ten years ago of the risk of passivity and indifference, an undeniable consequence of the collapse of total syntheses. Perhaps some or many men need to believe in an absolute, in radical transformation, for even partial reforms to be achieved. Perhaps ideological eloquence and utopian visions are the necessary counterpart to rationalization and an antidote to the disheartening objectivity of experts, especially in our technological society. We would, nevertheless, be ill advised to condemn the pragmatism of the "social engineers" while asserting the "practical necessity" for a "total interpretation of the world"; I know of no more contemptible form of pragmatism than that practiced by certain privileged persons who try to propagate a faith they do not share: bourgeois who want a religion for the people, intellectuals who are afraid of spreading despair among the workers of Billancourt by revealing the truth about the Soviet Union, or Westerners who preach the gospel of "total interpretation" to underdeveloped countries that are of necessity provincial because of their technical and scientific backwardness.

This said, I willingly leave to others the no doubt essential task of infusing passion into political controversies—even those that belong in the realm of scientific investigation; I agree that henceforth the stress should be not so much on the technological aspects as on the moral and political aspects of these controversies. I agree to this all the more readily since the reaction against extreme forms of pragmatism leads to a valuable, if commonplace, discovery—namely, that the link between a vision and the will to achieve it, between facts and values, is characteristic of all committed political thinking, perhaps of *all* political thinking.

III

If we criticize ideological syntheses, does this mean that we are left helpless, without hope or guidance, in a historical situation deprived of meaning? Does it mean that political philosophy is bankrupt? I would like to show that this is by no means the case.

Ideological skepticism, which is not the same as moral or philosophical skepticism, admittedly includes an element of what is called (especially in English-speaking countries) conservatism. This explains why critics tend to interpret the revolt against ideology as a new version of conservatism. But what anti-ideologists borrow from conservatism* is a part of general human wisdom: societies are complex entities, men are not

* Need I say that I do not regard the term as pejorative?

creatures of pure reason, and principles such as equality and liberty either are defined in abstract terms and give rise to controversial arguments as soon as any attempt is made to embody them in institutions, or else are defined explicitly in which case they have no more than a historical significance. We do not know what the future holds in store, and although we are entitled to imagine the society of our dreams or fears, how can we fail to realize that "men create their own history but know not the history they create"?

Are we therefore doomed to the fashionable malady of "alienation"? Must an intellectual without a total system of interpretation of the historical world resign himself to alienation, becoming himself the prisoner of an idea, but of an idea that condemns him to inaction?

The word "alienation" has crossed the Atlantic, and Americans, with their thirst for ideology, have fallen eagerly on this vestige of the Hegelian-Marxist tradition. The term has finally taken on so wide and vague a meaning that any dissatisfaction or disparity between an individual's aspirations and the conditions imposed on him by his environment is said to be alienation. It goes without saying that we are all "alienated," not because we are robbed of our essence or our humanity, but because—involved as we are in complex organizations, living within the framework of a social order that belongs to us but resists our desires—we have countless opportunities of failing to achieve self-recognition and can no longer tell whether this condition—this kind of existence—was inevitable or willed. If, into the bargain, we are intellectuals, we also recognize the fragmentation of culture and the esoteric nature of the arts and sciences as an additional form of "alienation." We find ourselves shut off in a narrow sector of a world whose entirety cannot be grasped by any one person. By what miracle could one single "ideology" combine in one whole all of our fragmented knowledge, the range of which is widened every day by the efforts of thousands or millions of research workers? The synthesis of Marxism-Leninism is a mockery. As for "immortal principles," they may serve as a guide for action, but they cannot recreate the paradise of lost unity.

I listed earlier the four elements of the argument between the Soviets and the West as it is now pursued: the economic issue concerning respective merits of market economies and centralized planning; the political, social, and human consequences of the different systems; the contrast between the two patterns of historical development; and the effort to discover the ultimate goal of industrial societies. As long as the conflict continued between the affirmation and denial (both dogmatic) of total ideologies, differentiation among these levels was impossible and no dialogue could take place.

As regards the second issue, the political and social consequences of a given economic system, the debate has an essentially philosophical character. Two arguments especially relate to the essence of the good society: one is the plurality of parties and philosophies vs. a single-party system and intellectual orthodoxy; the other, an individualist conception vs. a collectivist conception of existence. Both systems claim to be democratic: power emanates from the proletariat; the man in the street, the common man, the worker—these are in theory the political sovereigns to whom the leaders address themselves and with whose lot they claim to be chiefly concerned. But the methods of selecting political rulers, and the ways in which the systems function, are and will probably remain profoundly different. They cannot be judged solely with reference to efficiency (itself measured in terms of growth of production or productivity). The political system of the Soviet Union, the single-party system, is bound up with an authoritarian philosophy of power and a Communist philosophy of existence. A few minds may still cling to the utopia of a final anarchy, but this is no longer even an inspirational myth; it is an alibi, or a camouflage of reality.

This brings us back to a traditional theme of political philosophy: the relationship between the individual and the community, and between society and the state. To maintain that a market economy increases man's sense of isolation and that only a planned economy is able to give him a sense of participation is to present a crude version of a genuine problem. The question is: what kind of system encourages social integration? And what kind of social integration do we think desirable? Can, or must, the worker be fulfilled in his work? Can he and does he want to be a member of the community formed by his industrial unit? Or is it the function of technological and economic progress to free men from the pressure of necessity, which has always been part of the very nature of labor?

The breakdown of ideological syntheses does not lead to insipid pragmatism or lessen the value of intellectual controversy. On the contrary, it encourages a return to rational discussion of problems which, in any case, must be solved pragmatically, and lays bare the eternal and conflicting aspirations in the hearts of men and in the turmoil of history.

The reason why the rejection of total ideologies is often confused with the denial of any kind of political philosophy is a simple one: this rejection is itself an expression of a certain kind of philosophy, and representatives of other schools of thought do not recognize it as being what they themselves think of as philosophy.

We think and act in history—that is, in particular combinations of circumstances and according to values that vary in their concrete expression even if, at a certain level of abstract formulation, they may be termed eternal or universal. What a society demands in the name of freedom—the kind of equality held essential for humanizing interpersonal relationships, in other words, the content of the abstract concepts—belongs to the realm of history. This content may be arranged in some sort of order, but this will not necessarily imply evolution; it is not as if the concepts became enriched with the passing of time and lost nothing of their former value, or as if the historical succession of various types of society must inevitably culminate in a final reconciliation of them all. There is no option that does not involve sacrifices, there is no system that does not include features one would like to see eradicated. Even a system that completely fulfilled its aims would exclude some attainments we should prefer to keep. Leaving aside the contradictions between the specific values of different worlds (a thing may be beautiful because it is immoral)—what Weber called the conflict between the gods—a political, economic, or social system, like a language, includes certain possibilities and excludes others. Anyone who thinks he can embrace the whole of history forgets these contradictions, which define the historical condition of man. Whether he claims to obey objective laws of history or puts his trust in the Promethean possibilities of knowledge and reason, he disregards the limitations of man's knowledge and power, individual or collective, and rejects what is sometimes called the tragic nature of our collective destiny. In a completely rationalized society, the masses would be controlled by a small group of men devoid of illusion. If the bonds woven by tradition and faith were ever finally broken, the event would not mark the triumph of reason, but of technology.

Perhaps a brief comparison with a number of Herbert Marcuse's ideas will make clearer my own concept of a philosophy that adopts a critical approach to history without being "total" or advocating a state of things radically different from the one in which we live.

Marcuse recognizes—and even asserts—that reason no longer tends to exercise its function of total negation. He admits that the decline of radical criticism is an exact expression of contemporary reality: "Under such conditions, decline of freedom and opposition is not a matter of moral or intellectual deterioration or corruption. It is rather an objective societal process insofar as the production and distribution of an increasing quantity of goods and services make compliance a rational technological attitude." * Radical criticism and negative reasoning have ceased to be embodied in history since in highly developed industrial societies the proletariat has ceased to be revolutionary. Yet reality has not become rational; extreme irrationality has taken on the semblance of technological rationality (or, if you prefer, technical rationality, left to itself, led to irrationality). Alienation seems to have disappeared, since individuals identify themselves with their existence as it takes place objectively. But identification of this kind, although real and not illusory, is nonetheless a further stage of alienation. Man is no longer aware of his own alienation and allows himself to be absorbed in his alienated existence.

Perhaps the following passage contains the most clearly defined expression of Marcuse's analysis of history:

> The critical theory of society was, at the time of its origin, confronted with the presence of real forces (objective and subjective) *in* the established society which moved (or could be

* *One Dimensional Man* (Boston: Beacon Press, 1964), p. 48.

guided to move) toward more rational and freer institutions by abolishing the existing ones which had become obstacles to progress. These were the empirical grounds on which the theory was erected, and from these empirical grounds derived the idea of the liberation of *inherent* possibilities—the development, otherwise blocked and distorted, of material and intellectual productivity, faculties, and needs.*

Without the demonstration of such forces, the critique of society, while still valid and rational, would be incapable of translating its rationality into terms of historical practice. "The conclusion? 'Liberation of inherent possibilities' no longer adequately expresses the historical alternative." The weapon of criticism and the criticism of weapons, the philosophical rejection of reality and the revolutionary determination of the proletariat, the head and the heart of the revolution are no longer bound together. Thus, society appears rational because it is accepted, and rejection seems empty since it is unable to define its own content. Yet both Western and Soviet societies are irrational to the very core.

What does this irrationality consist of, and how can it be demonstrated, in the absence of historical opposition to it? Without attempting to summarize in a few pages Marcuse's complex and often obscure indictment, I should like to give the gist of a few of his charges. Sovietism is no more kindly treated than capitalism, although the former perhaps offers a better outlook for the future and the latter offers better guarantees for the time being.† Both systems are irrational. The in-

* Ibid., pp. 254-55.

† "Still, for the administered individual, pluralistic administration is far better than total administration. One institution might protect him against the other; one organization might mitigate the impact of the other; possibilities of escape and redress can be calculated. The rule of law, no matter how restricted, is still infinitely safer than rule above or without law."

ternal irrationality of each is exacerbated by the fact that each is engaged in a struggle with the other.

Preparations for a nuclear war in which millions of men would perish, and the calculation of the possible number of victims of such a war illustrate the combination of technological progress and lunacy that is characteristic of our day and age. Billions of dollars are devoted each year to the preparation for armed conflict, while two-thirds of humanity live in bitter poverty and, in the more advanced countries, many if not most people are condemned to drudgery and poverty.

Irrational because they use their productive potential to prepare for the most monstrous kind of destruction known to history, modern industrial societies are also (at least in the West) irrational in that they create false needs but do not satisfy the true needs of the entire population, as they might; they limit the leisure that each individual might enjoy and, above all, manipulate human minds so as to prevent them understanding and realizing what genuine self-determination would be.

For the most part, except for the terms in which it is phrased, this indictment is not original. It is not an accident that Marcuse should quote in his introduction books normally considered as popularized critiques on the irrationalities of American civilization—Vance Packard's *The Hidden Persuaders, The Status Seekers* and *The Waste Makers,* William H. Whyte's *The Organization Man,* Fred J. Cook's *The Warfare State.* These books do indeed portray a society in which the population is swayed by mass media, obedient to the commands of the major vested interests. Because they are indoctrinated by the mass media, the people want the goods offered them, vote for the candidates they are advised to vote for, like or dislike whatever publicity or propaganda teaches them to like or dislike, and in the end forget the very nature of freedom. "The growing productivity of labor creates an increasing surplus-product which, whether privately or centrally appropriated and distributed, allows an increased consumption— notwithstanding the increased diversion of productivity. As long as this constellation prevails, it reduces the use-value of freedom; there is no reason to insist on self-determination if the administered life is the comfortable and even the 'good' life." *

This radical critique is, in fact, many-sided and heterogeneous. It combines a criticism of the socio-economic structure (the workers do not decide their own fate but are controlled either by the big corporations or by the single party of the totalitarian state); a criticism of mass society, controlled by the mass media; a criticism of waste (the resources provided by increased productivity are used to satisfy false needs); a criticism of violence, which continues to characterize the struggle for existence on both sides of the Iron Curtain; and finally a criticism of the rivalry between the two hostile systems, which will either provoke the catastrophe of a thermonuclear war or be prolonged indefinitely for the sole purpose of justifying permanent mobilization and the continuance of the authority that holds the people in subjection.

What Marcuse calls the Great Refusal can, therefore, in my view, be split up into a series of critiques each one of which is open to discussion. It is not without irony that a critique of society obviously deriving from Marx should have as its supreme aim the pacification of human relations, while admitting its inability to achieve this. "The critical theory of society possesses no concepts which could bridge the gap between the present and its future; holding no promise and showing no suc-

* *Ibid.,* p. 49.

cess, it remains negative. Thus it wants to remain loyal to those who, without hope, have given and give their life to the Great Refusal." * I am not sure that there is such an enormous difference between the Great Refusal, which is without hope and impossible to realize, and universal resignation.

History—as it has actually occurred and not as Marxists or idealists imagined it—has cured some of the ills denounced by those who lived during the industrial revolution of the nineteenth century. It has also failed to realize some of the hopes they entertained. Under private and public ownership, production and productivity go on increasing and the living standards of the masses rise accordingly. In this sense, reality has outstripped fiction. Both defenders and critics of the capitalism of fifty years ago would be astonished at the material results it has achieved. (These results are perhaps inferior to what technological advance has made possible, but no society has ever fully realized its own potential.) Even the theoretician of the Great Refusal has little doubt that industrial societies are capable of gradually eliminating the isolated patches of poverty and undeserved misfortune that are still found in the midst of opulence.

Nevertheless, the development of production has not abolished the exploitation of man by man or, if we prefer to avoid that ambiguous term, the dominance of man over man. A rationalized society is a graded society, in which the greatest number meekly accept their fate. If we start from the utopian idea that men, both singly and as a community, should choose their own destiny, modern society appears increasingly oppressive, authoritarian, and totalitarian as it becomes more industrialized. Within each business or firm, there can be no relaxa-

* *Ibid.,* p. 257.

tion of discipline, since more often than not the worker performs his duties without realizing or understanding the nature of the total entity to which he belongs. This state of affairs will persist as long as the main objective is to produce as much as possible, as efficiently as possible. The Great Refusal cannot be a refusal of productivity, since it aims to free man from the slavery of work. If it fails to impinge on history, this is because it invokes the principle of self-determination, which is so abstract as to be almost devoid of meaning.

Freedom in work will always be restricted by the demands imposed by efficiency, by the inevitable authority of technical experts or directors. Freedom to achieve self-realization in leisure pursuits depends on the potentiality of each individual. He will be molded by the entertainment industries or will resist collective persuasion according to whether his inner life is strong or weak, and whether he is protected by his education or vulnerable through having failed in his youth to acquire the training necessary for individual accomplishment. Whether we refer to work or leisure pursuits, self-determination is no more than an ideal (in the pejorative sense in which Marx would have understood the term), since the individual who appeals to it is incapable of saying what institutions would make it possible in practice. In diverse means and by partial measures, such as reforming industrial organization or broadening the educational system, we can humanize the power wielded by the administrators of collective enterprises and give each individual a better opportunity to choose his own career. But we cannot arrange things so that an industrial society—that is, a rationally administered one—corresponds to the impulses of anarchistic individualism. For the administration of material things to cease to be the government of people—and this seems to be one of the utopian ideals Marcuse advances*—people would have to lead leisurely and solitary existences. Between big corporations of the American type and the single-party system, many intermediary possibilities are conceivable, and some of them in fact exist; they will not escape condemnation in the light of the "critical theory of society."

Providing the concept of irrationality were replaced by that of unreasonableness, I would willingly subscribe to some of Marcuse's judgments on our times, although his point of view is that of a detached, indeed otherworldly, observer. There *is* an element of truth (difficult to assess) in the (hackneyed) denunciation of artificial needs and the abuses of publicity; it is not untrue that the mass media help to stimulate demands without which the productive machinery would be threatened with paralysis. It is possible to imagine an industrial society that attempted to satisfy everyone's vital needs before satisfying the artificial needs of the few. But no society known to history has avoided injustice, luxury for the privileged few, and poverty for the majority. What is new is that the luxury enjoyed by the few does not prevent improvement for the masses.† It is possible to wish for more and, by a series of reforms, to obtain more, but, so far, no economic or political system has succeeded in gaining sufficient control over social mechanisms to ensure that resources are distributed among the various members of the community according to reasonable priorities.

Similarly, it is easy to imagine a society that would not al-

---

* Another utopian idea is to make the workers themselves responsible for the administration of industry.

† The reference is again to developed societies.

low itself to be swept along by the dynamic force of science, production, and productivity. Competitive rates of growth, the arms race, and the ambition to send astronauts to the moon are all excessive, frenzied, and, if you like, unreasonable phenomena. Life for the majority of human beings could be less harsh if only the various states would agree to limit population growth, control arms, and distribute wealth more evenly. Henri Bergson, too, believed that pacification was incompatible with the mad desire for consumption and enjoyment. It can even be legitimately argued that in the overdeveloped countries the sheer quantity of goods, services, work, and recreation limits freedom and that qualitative change would involve "reduction of overdevelopment." *

However, the industrial society is still only in its initial phase. It has been no more successful in eliminating injustice and inequality than in abolishing the division of humanity into sovereign states. As long as this division remains, so will the race for knowledge and power. Total rejection of the fragmented world of the present is a sterile attitude and degenerates into a kind of obscurantism. It is easy to make ironical comments on the operations of the Rand Corporation and the application of game theory to the uncertainties of diplomacy, but it is the responsibility of statesmen to see that the threat of atomic warfare is never translated into reality. Given the present state of the world, it is not within their power to remove the threat of atomic war from international relations as if by miracle. Why should reflection on the powerful nature of modern weapons and the subtleties of dissuasion not help them to discover means of reducing the dangers to which humanity has become exposed through its very conquests?

* Ibid., p. 242.

The critical theory of society suffers from an internal contradiction. It deplores the absence of radical negation, yet at the same time it adopts the pacification of human relations as its supreme ideal. The Great Refusal has never been considered as a call to peace. If in present circumstances the Great Refusal is not bellicose, this is in fact because it takes its stand outside history, not in it.

Radical criticism has abandoned the attempt to re-think the world or to change it; it is content to condemn.

What paralyzes utopian thought and stifles dreams of a millenium in the West is not so much ignorance of the future as knowledge of the present. Marx, writing during the initial phase of industrialization, could both ruthlessly criticize a system that was a cruel one for most people and leave the task of reconciling man with his destiny (or, to put it another way, of overcoming the various "alienations") to the expansion of productive forces, to public ownership, and to the proletarian revolution. The development of productive forces has surpassed Marxian expectations; it has not, even in the most modernized countries, put an end to the dialectics of man and his achievements, the very stuff of history. Anti-ideology as I conceived it ten years ago and as I still see it today means accepting this dialectical conflict and being resigned, not to present forms of "alienation," but to the endless renewal of alienation in some form or other.

We are more fortunate than previous generations in that we are not forced to make a choice between conservatism and fanaticism, i.e., between the defense of the status quo and a kind of blindness that is alternately humanitarian and bloody. We know that modern methods—scientific and technological progress and the rational organization of labor—enable us to achieve the objectives to which liberals and socialists of previous centuries aspired. We know, on the abstract level at least, how to attain them. The advanced countries of the West have or will have the necessary resources to ensure a decent standard of living for everyone, and they will not be forced to sacrifice personal liberties in order to ensure this spread of material prosperity.

It goes without saying that abundance brings disappointment. Even if we disregard the two-thirds of humanity who are still far from enjoying plenty and ignore the darker areas of life in the more fortunate nations, the fact remains that rationalized society is still hierarchical and torn by national or racial passions. When such passions die down, they are in danger of being replaced by bourgeois complacency. Intellectuals who are inclined to criticize, and that means almost all intellectuals, denounce both the threat of an atomic war and the passivity of television viewers indoctrinated by the entertainment industry or the totalitarian state. They refuse to recognize the socialism of their youth either in the monstrosities of Stalinism, in the more normal despotism of his successors, or in America's society of big corporations and mass culture. They are right to be dissatisfied with the imperfections of reality and to criticize the injustice of certain institutions and the mediocrity of most men's lives. But whether they want to do so or not, they are in fact unable to set up against existing society the image of a radically different one. Scientific progress, technological advance, and increasing productivity are part and parcel of the industrial type of society whose evolution moves ineluctably toward a future we cannot foresee. But the philosopher is not the prophet. At the present time, prognostication and anticipation of future needs are fashionable: both practices correspond to the needs of a constantly changing civilization. Scientific and technological progress is our destiny; we try to predict what it will do to us, and we sometimes tend to forget to ask ourselves what we would like to make of it. It is no less important to examine our own intentions.

Here, no doubt, we come to the crux of the matter. It is possible to think of two ways that the ideological dispute might be revived. Until recently, ideologies sanctified methods or institutions that we today tend to judge primarily in terms of their efficiency. Such ideologies can be revived, perhaps, by applying them to countries at the stage of development corresponding to the West's at the time when these ideologies were formulated or in their hey-day. I doubt, however, that such a process can prove fruitful.

No society of the past has ever possessed so much knowledge about itself as we have about ours. Statistics can tell us the present size of a given population, its probable size in ten or twenty years' time, and the per-capita national product at various periods in accordance with the rate of economic growth. What influence can a philosopher's logical discourse hope to have on a country where a comparison of demographic and economic growth rates makes it possible to forecast an indefinite continuance of poverty? In an age when a decent standard of living for all is considered prerequisite of the good society, institutions and systems are inevitably judged in relation to the primary demands of expansion, and the judgment is bound to be pragmatic rather than moral or philosophical.

Let us go further. For any reflective observer, history from now to the end of the century will be dominated by two facts: the hydrogen bomb and the population explosion. This is not to say that the earth will be unable to provide food for six or seven billion people by the year 2,000, even without an acceleration in the present rate of food production. A thermonuclear war would not necessarily end the human species, nor would the inhabitants of an overpopulated world be doomed to mutual destruction. But the material and moral disasters that might result from either a thermonuclear war or a too rapid rise in the world birth rate are such that it is difficult not to be obsessed by them. There is no longer any common measure between the consequences of a thermonuclear war or the possible tripling of the world population and the scope of political party quarrels. However, there is one way of instilling fresh life into Western ideas while at the same time perhaps indirectly helping underdeveloped areas: this is to try and discover the meaning of the historical phase we are now living in. At the present time, economic growth is for some countries a categorical imperative because it is a necessary condition for survival. For all countries, even the advanced ones, it is an essential means for the achievement of any aim. It cannot in itself be an ultimate aim. Our Western societies themselves sometimes appear not to know what they propose to do with their wealth and power.

The confrontation between Communism and the West, which prompts some superficial observers to prophesy a *rapprochement* and reconciliation between the two systems in some kind of democratic socialism, shows, on the contrary, that the same volume of resources can be shared out in entirely different ways—i.e., used to consolidate power or achieve material prosperity—and, furthermore, that social organization can aim either at the absorption of the individual into an entirely state-controlled society or, on the contrary, at the widening of the individual's margin of initiative. At any stage of development, the collectivism-individualism dilemma retains its significance because industrialization can be oriented toward either. Similarly, on a political level, human liberties will never be guaranteed by prosperity; the single-party system and the indoctrination of the masses are and will remain threats or temptations.

Philosophical discourse, unlike historical mythologies, does not reveal the secret of collective salvation or the means of miraculously eliminating what critics of society judge to be irrational—racial passions, national prejudices, petty-bourgeois mediocrity, the vulgarity of mass culture, the arms race, threats of atomic war. On the other hand, it does not teach discouragement; although men as a whole have never experienced the satisfaction of self-achievement in common effort, and although there is no proof that total, unanimous self-realization of this kind is possible, humanity is henceforth in possession of material means, undreamed-of a few years ago, that allow it to forge its own destiny. But this power may be used for evil just as much as for good.

The task of the philosopher who sets out to be a teacher of wisdom is more exhilarating today than ever before. But would it be right to assure men that they are already wise, or that history will relieve them of the obligations of wisdom?

About the Author

RAYMOND ARON is Professor of Sociology at the University of Paris and Director of Studies at the École Pratique des Hautes Études.

He is the author of *The Great Debate*, *The Dawn of Universal History*, *France: the New Republic*, *German Sociology*, *Introduction to the Philosophy of History*, *The Opium of the Intellectuals*, and *Peace and War: A Theory of International Relations*.